Everyman
and
Medieval Miracle Plays

EDITED WITH AN INTRODUCTION BY
A. C. CAWLEY, M.A., PH.D.

*Professor of English Language
and Medieval English Literature in the University of Leeds*

J. M. Dent & Sons Ltd
LONDON, MELBOURNE AND TORONTO
E. P. Dutton & Co. Inc., NEW YORK

No. 381   Hardback ISBN 0 460 10381 4
No. 1381   Paperback ISBN 0 460 11381 x

PREFACE

THIS volume contains the moral play *Everyman* and a representative collection of medieval biblical pageants. The pageants have been chosen for their intrinsic merit and because together they give a fair idea of the range and content of an English Corpus Christi cycle. They are taken from the cycles of York, Chester, Wakefield, Coventry, and 'N. town,' with the addition of an excerpt from the Cornish plays (Appendix I). The Brome play of *Abraham and Isaac* is not, strictly speaking, a cyclic pageant; yet it resembles the cyclic pageants on the same theme and is superior to them.

Most of the original words of the plays are preserved, but for the convenience of the general reader many archaic forms and spellings are modernized or normalized both within the line and in rhyme. Occasionally, however, an archaic form is kept for the sake of the rhyme, and a gloss added if necessary. Original stage directions are given and those in Latin are translated; they are distinguished from editorial directions, which are bracketed. Difficult words and short phrases are glossed in the margin, while longer word-groups needing explanation are paraphrased in footnotes.

The Introduction and the forewords to the individual plays will serve as guides to further reading, if the books and articles referred to by their authors' surnames are identified in the Bibliography.

During the past twenty years there has been a considerable revival of interest in medieval English drama. In 1947 E. K. Chambers felt obliged to write: 'It is difficult to arrive at any very clear estimate of the literary value of plays which were never intended to be read, and cannot be given life by the gestures and intonation of the actors.'[1] But since he wrote these words there have been several productions of the cycles of York, Chester and Wakefield as well as of the 'N. town' and Cornish plays. As a result, we are now in a position to think of the plays as drama, as pieces of literature to be acted and completed on the stage. This in turn has encouraged the study both of the plays as dramatic literature and of the methods of staging them in medieval times.

[1] E. K. Chambers, *English Literature at the Close of the Middle Ages* (Oxford, 1947), p. 27.

v

The earlier scholars, who were perhaps inevitably preoccupied with the text and with textual problems, did excellent work on which all subsequent critical appraisal of the plays has been based. Some of them, however, regarded a medieval play as if it were a quaint, archaic onion, to be peeled off layer by layer, so that successive levels of composition by different authors could be revealed. This tedious operation usually compelled us to admire the scholar's ingenuity rather than the playwright's. Happily, more recent studies such as those by Arnold Williams, V. A. Kolve, and Rosemary Woolf have firmly led us back to the religious meaning and dramatic interest of the text; rightly so, for the primary concern of the medieval playwright was to instruct his audience through dramatic entertainment on the stage.

The second kind of activity stimulated by modern productions —the study of medieval methods of staging—is represented at its best by Richard Southern's book on the medieval theatre in the round and by Glynne Wickham's *Early English Stages*.

A related kind of study which has flourished over the past two decades involves the intensive use of new and old documentary material—civic, guild and church records from York, Chester, Newcastle, Lincolnshire and East Anglia—for the purpose of throwing light on the production of medieval plays. It has been much debated whether the plays at York and Wakefield were acted processionally or in one place; the debate goes on, adding zest to the study of medieval drama from Berkeley to New York and from Toronto to Sydney.

Last but not least, the parallels between drama and medieval iconography have been explored by art historians like M. Schapiro, W. L. Hildburgh and M. D. Anderson who have enlarged upon the distinguished work of Emile Mâle.

All these are international activities in which scholars of many different countries have taken part. Thanks to their efforts, we can no longer be superior or patronizing in our attitude to the medieval playwright; but we can now honestly admire his blending of sacred and secular themes and his handling of the stage conventions by which he conveys these themes to the eyes and ears of his audience and still more to their imagination.

Note: I should like to express my gratitude to Professor T.W. Craik, of the University of Dundee, for his corrections included in this revised edition.

A. C. C.

The University of Leeds,
   January, 1974.

INTRODUCTION

APART from *Everyman* and the excerpt representing the Cornish drama, the plays in this volume are biblical pageants [1] which are ultimately derived, like their counterparts in France, Spain, and Italy, from the Latin liturgical plays of the medieval Church.[2] They are religious in origin and inspiration no less than the church architecture, painting, and sculpture of the Middle Ages. It is a far cry from a tenth-century Latin trope for Easter, which was the beginning of liturgical drama, to the vernacular *Resurrection* pageant of the fifteenth-century York cycle, or from a simple Christmas trope to the sophisticated *Second Shepherds' Pageant* of Wakefield. But during the four or five centuries separating the Easter and Christmas tropes from the York and Wakefield pageants all the dramatic traditions, religious and secular, of the Middle Ages had had time to converge and so enrich the parent stock of the liturgical drama.

Nothing much remains of the secular drama of the Middle Ages: the most notable survivals, both fragmentary, are a fourteenth-century interlude *de Clerico et Puella* [3] and a fifteenth-century Robin Hood play.[4] The first of these, which no doubt belonged to the repertory of the minstrels, seems to preserve something of the traditions of classical comedy.

---

[1] Most of them are Corpus Christi pageants or guild pageants, i.e. short plays acted by the trade guilds as episodes of the whole Corpus Christi cycle. Municipal and craft records of the fifteenth and sixteenth centuries commonly distinguish between the individual 'pageant' and the 'Corpus Christi play' of which it formed part. In this Introduction the meaning of the word 'pageant' is usually thus restricted, while 'miracle play' (in the title of the book and elsewhere) has the general meaning of 'a vernacular religious play acted outside the church.' The medieval word 'miracle' is preferred to 'mystery,' which was first applied to English religious drama in 1744.

[2] The liturgical plays were acted in church as an integral part of the Divine Service. They grew out of the tropes, or chanted Latin dialogues, added to the service of the Mass at Easter and Christmas (see below, pp. 79, 171). For the development of European liturgical drama see Young and Hardison; for the transition from Latin liturgical plays to vernacular religious drama see Kolve and Woolf.

[3] Ed. Dickins and Wilson.

[4] Ed. Manly, Adams.

The medieval Robin Hood plays, represented by the second fragment, may also have been written and acted by minstrels; their origins are obscure, but it is known that they became inseparable from the May Day revels of the people. There is no extant example of a medieval St George play, and yet it is likely enough that the St George plays so often mentioned in medieval account-books are the ancestors of our mummers' plays, in some of which the legend of St George is grafted on to the theme of a symbolic death and resurrection.[1] The records of the medieval folk-play, meagre though they are, show that secular plays once had a share in the seasonal revels of the people. There is other evidence, mainly drawn from clerical Latin records of the twelfth and thirteenth centuries, which points to the existence in these centuries of theatres dedicated to the production of secular drama.[2]

The minor clerics also had their seasonal revels. The most notorious of these—the Feast of Fools, celebrated by the sub-deacons on the Feast of the Circumcision with all kinds of unseemly burlesque ceremonies—is thought to be a survival of the Kalends of January.[3] A less riotous celebration of the equality of man was the ceremony of the Boy Bishop, often held on Holy Innocents' Day, in which the choir-boys assumed for a brief period the duties and dignities of their clerical superiors.[4]

All these seasonal festivities may well have contributed something to the emotional depth as well as surface liveliness of the miracle plays. For example, the fondness of the Church for dramatizing the Easter Resurrection play may reflect the influence of the ritualistic folk-play.[5] Certainly, the symbolic death and resurrection of folk-drama and Christ's death and resurrection are parallel themes which could hardly fail to coalesce and influence each other.[6] Again, the folk

[1] For the mumming plays see Chambers, i. 205–27; also Beatty, Brody.
[2] Loomis and Cohen; cf. Wilson, *The Lost Literature of Medieval England*, p. 239, for Bishop Grandisson of Exeter's condemnation in 1352 of a 'certain noxious and blameworthy play, or rather buffoonery' acted by the leather-dressers.
[3] Chambers, i. 274–335.
[4] Chambers, i. 336–71.
[5] Beatty, p. 324; cf. Pascal, pp. 383–4.
[6] This is chronologically possible, for although the mummers' plays are preserved in late and often very corrupt texts there is no reason to doubt their antiquity. For the folklore elements in medieval drama see Axton; for the influence of pre-Christian ritual on the Wakefield pageants see Speirs, and cf. E. O. James, pp. 268 ff.

spirit of revelry has clearly left its mark on the *Second Shepherds' Pageant*, with its burlesque of the Nativity.

The coalescence of religious and secular, Christian and pagan, traditions produced in the fifteenth century a vernacular religious drama with a strong infusion of humorous and popular elements. Nevertheless this drama remained fundamentally religious in subject and inspiration, so that as late as the sixteenth century it was possible for William Newhall to write concerning the Chester play:

> Forasmuch as of old time, not only for the augmentation and increase of the holy and catholic faith of our Saviour, Jesu Christ, and to exhort the minds of common people to good devotion and wholesome doctrine therof, but also for the commonwealth and prosperity of this City, a play and declaration of divers stories of the Bible, beginning with the Creation and Fall of Lucifer, and ending with the general judgment of the world, to be declared and played in the Whitsun week. . . .[1]

Notwithstanding any popular elements it may contain, the Chester cycle, like all the other English cycles of religious pageants, was conceived and 'controlled by a logic which was theologic.'[2] The dramatic cycles, like the Old and New Testament sequences in manuscript illuminations,[3] roof bosses,[4] and painted glass,[5] are not haphazard illustrations of the biblical narrative. Rather, they select for illustration the leading facts of the scheme of salvation—the Incarnation, Crucifixion, and Resurrection—and only those Old Testament episodes which to the medieval mind typified and prefigured them. The unity of biblical history, in which God has declared His purpose for mankind, means that the Old Testament is full of foreshadowings of the New. Thus, according to the medieval tradition of exegesis, the shepherd Abel is a type of Christ the Good Shepherd, Cain a type of the Jews, and the death of Abel at his hands prefigures Christ's Passion. This symbolic treatment of the story of Cain and Abel explains why the murder of Abel is sometimes associated with the Passion in ecclesiastical art.[6] But the Cain and Abel story

[1] Chambers, ii. 349; Wickham, i. 344.
[2] Rossiter, p. 51.
[3] e.g. in *Queen Mary's Psalter*, ed. Warner.
[4] The roof bosses in the nave of Norwich Cathedral; Cave, p. 202.
[5] The painted glass of Great Malvern Priory; Rushforth, p. 4.
[6] Tristram, ii. 59.

has spiritual as well as prophetic meanings. As interpreted
by St Augustine, it is the opening phase of the terrestrial
struggle between the heavenly and earthly cities:[1] Abel belongs
to the city of God, and his murderer is the founder of the
fleshly city. The conflict between God and sinful man,
which comes to a climax in pageants like *Cain and Abel* and
Noah's Flood, gives way for a moment to love and reconcilia-
tion in the Shepherds' Plays, but breaks out again with
brutality and suffering in *Herod the Great*, and goes on from
climax to climax in the *Buffeting*, the *Flagellation*, and the
Crucifixion. The struggle between God and erring man,
between the heavenly and earthly cities, will be unending
until the last days of this world; and it takes on meaning only
in relation to the central and culminating events of Christian
history—the Incarnation and the victory of Calvary. Christ's
spiritual victory over sin and death is symbolized by the
carrying of the Host in triumphal procession on Corpus
Christi Day; it is given a human and historical setting in the
Corpus Christi cycle, which dramatizes the whole Christian
scheme of salvation.[2]

The miracle plays became associated with Corpus Christi
Day after 1311 when the Corpus Christi festival was officially
recognized. The Latin liturgical plays were acted inside the
church as a part of the offices of the different seasons;[3] but
the vernacular miracle plays, which were not thus restricted,
were commonly acted at Whitsun or on Corpus Christi Day,
when the weather was most likely to be favourable for performance out of doors. The Corpus Christi play of York is
first heard of in 1376–7,[4] that of Beverley (no longer extant) in
1377.[5] By this time the municipal authorities were in general
charge of the play, with the trade guilds of the town financing
and producing the individual pageants of the complete Corpus
Christi cycle. It was arranged as far as possible that each
guild should act a pageant in which it could advertise the skills
of its trade; sometimes a lively sense of humour seems to have

---

[1] *The City of God*, trans. Healey, xv. 1–7 (Everyman's Library, No. 983).
[2] For the central meaning of the N. town cycle, or *Ludus Coventriae*,
see Fry.
[3] It should be remembered that Latin tropes and liturgical plays con-
tinued to play a part in the services of the Church long after the miracle
plays had established themselves.
[4] Sellers, p. 10.   [5] Chambers, ii. 339.

decided the allocation of pageants, e.g. at Chester, where the water-leaders and drawers in Dee acted *Noah's Flood* and the cooks the *Harrowing of Hell*.

It is known from municipal records and guild ordinances that cycles of biblical pageants were acted in Ireland,[1] Scotland,[2] and in many of the more prosperous towns of England. But all of them are now lost,[3] except for the cycles of Chester, York, and Wakefield (to which the Towneley cycle probably once belonged), an unidentified and unlocalized cycle known as the N. town cycle or *Ludus Coventriae*, two pageants from Coventry, and one from Newcastle and Norwich respectively.

The texts of the pageants, apart from the late transcripts of the Norwich and Newcastle pageants and the Coventry pageant of the Shearmen and Tailors, are preserved in manuscripts of the fifteenth and sixteenth centuries. The cycles in their present form are the product of successive revisions and inter-borrowings. For example, some of the Towneley pageants show imitation of, and even word-for-word borrowing from, certain pageants of the York cycle. The fifteenth-century manuscript containing the York cycle was compiled as a 'register': that is to say, it was an official copy of the texts of the individual pageants made for the use of the municipal authorities in their capacity as overseers of the whole Corpus Christi play.[4] Only two working copies of individual pageants have survived. These are the manuscripts of the Chester *Antichrist* and York *Incredulity of Thomas*,[5] which were probably used as prompt-books by the guilds responsible for producing the pageants.

In trying to discover how the English pageants were produced we are handicapped by possessing nothing comparable to a director's copy like the *Abregiés* of Mons, used for a performance of the *Mystère de la Passion* in 1501.[6] But it is

[1] Clark, chap. i.
[2] Mill.
[3] Wilson, *The Lost Literature of Medieval England*, pp. 222 ff., writes about the lost cycles once acted in such towns as Beverley, Lincoln, and London. He also brings together evidence from churchwardens' accounts, priory accounts, etc., of the performance of single plays, including saints' plays, in numerous towns and villages of medieval England.
[4] The manuscript of the Towneley cycle may also have been compiled as a register; see Greg, p. 293, and Frampton, pp. 686–9.
[5] Cawley, p. 48. [6] Frank, p. 163.

known that the cycles at Chester and York were acted processionally, probably under the influence of the Corpus Christi procession, and that each guild performed its pageant on a wagon which was moved from one station (or prearranged acting-place) to another. The only detailed description of a pageant-wagon and of the processional mode of presentation is that given by David Rogers in the *Breviary* of Chester history (1609):

They [the Chester pageants] were divided into 24 pageants or parts, according to the number of the Companies of the City, and every Company brought forth their pageant, which was the carriage or place which they played in. And yearly, before these were played, there was a man fitted for the purpose which did ride . . . upon St George's Day through the City, and there published the time and the matter of the plays in brief, which was called 'the reading of the banns.' They were played upon Monday, Tuesday, and Wednesday in Whitsun week.[1] And they first began at the Abbey gates; and when the first pageant was played at the Abbey gates, then it was wheeled from thence to the Pentice at the High Cross before the Mayor; and before that was done, the second came, and the first went into the Watergate Street, and from thence unto the Bridge Street, and so all, one after another, till all the pageants were played, appointed for the first day, and so likewise for the second and the third day. This pageant or carriage was a high place made like a house with two rooms, being open on the top; in the lower room they apparelled and dressed themselves, and in the higher room they played; and they stood upon six wheels.[2]

A lot of information can be gained from the records of the guilds, including those of Coventry, Norwich, and Hull, about properties and mechanical effects, costumes, and the payment of actors. The inventory of the Norwich Grocers' Company (1565), which acted the *Creation of Eve and Expulsion from Eden*, lists such items as

---

[1] Cf. York and Wakefield, where the pageants were normally acted on Corpus Christi Day, the actors assembling at 4.30 a.m. in York (Smith, p. xxxiv) and at 5 a.m. in Wakefield (Walker, i. 150).

[2] Greg and Salter, p. 146. It should be noticed, however, that many of the miracle plays were not processional but stationary in type, i.e. acted in one place, which might be a croft, close, or market square. At Newcastle, for example, the crafts first took part in the Corpus Christi procession and afterwards seem to have acted their pageants in a prearranged place or 'stead' (Welford, ii. 133; Chambers, ii. 385). For a survey of the problems of processional and stationary performance see Nagler, pp. 55–73.

A pageant, that is to say, a house of wainscot painted and builded on a cart with four wheels.

A square top to set over the said house.[1]

A griffon, gilt, with a fane to set on the said top.

A rib coloured red.

2 coats and a pair hosen for Eve, stained.

A coat and hosen for Adam, stained.

A face [mask] and hair [wig] for the Father.

2 hairs for Adam and Eve.[2]

But the properties were not always so simple as 'A rib coloured red.' The records of the Coventry Smiths' Company (c. 1469) mention:

The cross with a rope to draw it up and a curtain hanging before it, two pair of gallows, four scourges and a pillar . . . a standard of red buckram; two red pensils [streamers] of cloth painted and silk fringe, iron to hold up the streamer.[3]

Curious mechanical effects were also used, as can be seen from the following items in the records of the Coventry Drapers' Company (c. 1534):

Hell-mouth—a fire kept at it; windlass and three fathom of cord; earthquake, barrel for the same . . . three worlds painted . . . a link to set the world on fire.[4]

The coats and hose for Adam and Eve, listed in the Norwich inventory, were presumably tight-fitting costumes of white leather representing the nakedness of Adam and Eve after the Fall. Symbolism in costume was not uncommon: the Coventry torturers wore 'jackets of black buckram . . . with nails and dice upon them.'[5] Otherwise the actors wore contemporary dress; for example, the high priests Caiaphas and Annas had 'mitres' and 'a bishop's tabard of scarlet.'[6]

The accounts of the Trinity House guild of master mariners and pilots at Hull include the following payments to performers in their *Noah* pageant on Plough Monday in 1483:

To the minstrels, 6d.

To Noah and his wife, 1s. 6d.

To Robert Brown playing God, 6d.[7]

[1] This reference to a roof for the pageant-wagon seems to belie Rogers' statement (p. xii) that the carriage was 'open on the top.' However, the words 'open on the top' are ambiguous, and may rather mean that the upper room (i.e. the stage proper) was open to view, while the lower room was not.

[2] Chambers, ii. 388.

[3] Craig, *Two Coventry Corpus Christi Plays*, p. 82.

[4] Ibid., p. 99.   [5] Ibid., p. 88.   [6] Ibid., p. 86.

[7] Chambers, ii. 370. For the significance of payments to actors see Wickham, *The Medieval Theatre*, p. 91.

The actors were worthy of their hire if all the authorities, like those at York, insisted on their being 'sufficient in person and cunning [ability].' [1]

Further information about the staging of the pageants can be gleaned from a study of the visual arts, some of which may have been influenced by the dramatic representation of biblical scenes and persons. Certainly, the use of a balcony to represent heaven and of gaping jaws to counterfeit the entrance to hell, as well as the gilded wigs worn by holy persons, are details common to the medieval religious stage and medieval religious imagery.[2]

Finally, the texts of the pageants and the original stage directions in many of them often localize a scene, name properties and costumes, or indicate the gestures and movements of the actors.[3] One interesting fact established by stage directions is the use of the street as an extension of the pageant-wagon, as when we are told in the Coventry Pageant of the Shearmen and Tailors that 'Here Herod rages in the pageant and in the street also.'

It is evident that the technique of the men who produced the pageants was largely derived from the staging of liturgical plays.[4] In the acting area were two or three fixed positions representing different localities, the space between being neutral ground except when it was localized by the words of the actors. By this method of simultaneous staging it was possible to suggest a change of scene without the actor having to do more than cross the stage from one position to another. The number of exits and entrances was thus reduced to a minimum, and in some of the pageants it is likely that all the actors were visible on different parts of the stage from the beginning to the end of the action. The use of music to heighten dramatic moments (e.g. the Chester stage direction *Minstrels play*, just after Cain has murdered Abel) is also an inheritance from liturgical drama, which was essentially music-drama.[5]

[1] Raine, p. 5.
[2] Hildburgh; Anderson, pp. 87–177; Nagler, pp. 89–105.
[3] See, for example, the original stage directions in the Chester *Noah's Flood* and in the N. town pageant of the *Woman taken in Adultery*.
[4] Nicoll, p. 69; Williams, p. 41.
[5] Smoldon, p. 175.

Very little is known about the authors of the miracle plays, although their familiarity with religious doctrine points to their clerical status. At Beverley a Dominican friar, Thomas Bynham, was commissioned to write the banns advertising the Corpus Christi play in 1423.[1] The names of a few other authors or revisers are known, e.g. Robert Croo, who corrected the Coventry Shearmen and Tailors' pageant in 1534.[2]

The Corpus Christi pageants seem to have kept their hold on the affections of the people up to the last days of the medieval religious stage. They were a communal activity affording doctrine and mirth to all classes of society: they were an important social occasion for a woman like the Wife of Bath, who enjoyed nothing better than to see and be seen; they gave an amateur actor like Absolon in the *Miller's Tale* the chance to show what he could do in the part of Herod; and they taught a man like Chaucer's carpenter [3] much of his biblical lore. When they finally came to an end in Elizabeth I's reign, it was not because they had lost their popularity, but because they were suppressed by Reformist zeal, reinforced by state opposition to their alleged 'idolatry and superstition.' [4]

The moral plays, represented in this volume by *Everyman*, are first heard of at about the same time as the guild pageants. The earliest recorded English play of this kind is the lost *Paternoster Play* of York, referred to in the English version of Wiclif's *De Officio Pastorali* (1378). Like the later moralities, the *Paternoster Play* evidently personified the vices and virtues.

The superficial differences between morality and biblical pageant are plain to see. The morality does not dramatize biblical persons and episodes, but personifies the good and bad qualities of Everyman and usually shows them in conflict. The pageant is a part of the whole cycle: it presents a phase in the spiritual history of mankind. The morality is complete in itself, and is restricted in scope to the spiritual biography of the microcosm Man. But, notwithstanding these differences, the moralities and biblical pageants have many points of contact. The use of allegorical figures is already found in the

[1] Leach, p. 215; Nelson, *The Medieval English Stage*, p. 93.
[2] Craig, *Two Coventry Corpus Christi Plays*, p. 31.
[3] In the *Miller's Tale*.
[4] Gardiner, pp. xi–xiii.

twelfth-century Advent play from Germany, *Antichristus*; and the sudden appearance of Death in *Everyman* is paralleled by the stealthy entrance of *Mors* in the N. town pageant of the *Death of Herod*. Again, both morality and cyclic pageant show the influence of the sermon [1] and of folk activities (the folk-play has left its mark on the moral play called *Mankind*,[2] just as the folk-tale has provided the comic episode of the *Second Shepherds' Pageant*). Both are less interested in man's earthly life than in his spiritual welfare in the life to come; both are vitally concerned with man in relation to his Creator. In short, both kinds of play are religious in meaning, and both have been humanized by popular influences.

The English moral plays preserved from the fifteenth century, despite their common characteristics, are strikingly different from each other in certain respects. Thus *Everyman* is distinguished from *Mankind* [3] by its consistent seriousness, from *Wisdom* [3] by its lack of interest in the contemporary scene, and from the *Castle of Perseverance* [3] by the economy and clarity of its language and construction. It is further distinguished from all of them by its preoccupation with death and its avoidance of any serious conflict between good and evil for the soul of Everyman. The dramatization of this conflict, which is handled so vigorously in the *Castle of Perseverance*, makes it the best of the moralities after *Everyman*.[4]

There is no longer any need to be hostile to the vernacular religious drama of the Middle Ages, or to be patronizing or squeamish about it. Historians of the drama like Chambers, Young, and Mantzius have demonstrated that four or five centuries of development lie behind the dramatic cycles of

---

[1] Owst, chap. viii.

[2] Smart, Brown, Axton.

[3] *The Macro Plays*, ed. Furnivall and Pollard, Eccles, Bevington. The manuscript of these plays is particularly interesting because it contains a diagram illustrating the production of the *Castle of Perseverance* (Bevington, *The Macro Plays*, p. 152). The acting area is circular in shape and surrounded by a ditch; inside the circle is the castle, and outside are directions for the positions of the actors' stations or scaffolds. The localization of heaven in the east and hell in the north preserves the orientation established in performances of liturgical plays. There are three similar plans for the Cornish plays (Furnivall and Pollard, pp. xxxiii–iv).

[4] For a survey of the moralities see Chambers, *English Literature at the Close of the Middle Ages*, pp. 49 ff., Craig, pp. 338 ff., and Potter.

Chester, York, and Wakefield.   If they are artless productions, they have no business to be.   In the past, students of medieval plays have been more interested in the textual problems they present than in their value as drama.   But the recent revivals of these cycles should help to stimulate an interest in the dramatic art of the biblical pageants.   The insight gained from performance is bound to lead to a fuller appreciation of the plays:

They are judged (in the study) to be crudely written Biblical scenes interspersed with occasional and unseemly knock-about.   But let anyone take the trouble to produce one, and he will see how deep a sense of worship can combine in the richly boisterous world of simple folk and Christian feeling.   It is as if laughter intensified the power to pray, as if the sublime could best be apprehended by those who are open to the ridiculous, as if Christianity were a thing so strong that it can include all the explosions of laughter a dramatist can devise.[1]

As for a moral play like *Everyman*, its lenten austerity can hardly fail to impress any but the most spiritually torpid.

Medieval religious drama is valuable not only for itself, but as a preparation for the golden age of English drama. The staging of the miracles and moralities (the use of a balcony, of unlocalized playing-space, mechanical effects, and music) and the freedom of the medieval playwrights in 'mingling kings and clowns'—all these things were a part of the heritage of the great Elizabethan dramatists.

[1] Coghill, p. 163.

SELECT BIBLIOGRAPHY

This list includes those books and articles referred to by their authors' surnames in the Introduction and in the foreword to each pageant.

ADAMS, J. Q., ed.: *Chief Pre-Shakespearean Dramas*, Boston, 1924.
ANDERSON, M. D.: *Drama and Imagery in English Medieval Churches*, Cambridge, England, 1963.
AXTON, R.: *European Drama of the Early Middle Ages*, London, 1974.
BEATTY, A.: 'The St George, or Mummers', Play: A Study in the Protology of the Drama,' *Transactions of the Wisconsin Academy of Sciences, Arts and Letters*, xv, part 2, 273–324 (1906).
BEVINGTON, D. M.: *From 'Mankind' to Marlowe: Growth of Structure*

in the Popular Drama of Tudor England, Cambridge, Mass., 1962; ed.: *The Macro Plays* (*The Castle of Perseverance, Wisdom, Mankind*): *A Facsimile Edition with Facing Transcriptions*, New York and Washington, D.C., 1972; ed.: *Medieval Drama*, Boston, 1975.

BLOCK, K. S., ed.: *Ludus Coventriae*, Early English Text Society, Extra Series, 120 (1922).

BRODY, A.: *The English Mummers and Their Plays*, London, 1971.

BROWN, A.: 'Folklore Elements in the Medieval Drama,' *Folk-Lore*, lxiii. 65–78 (1952).

CAVE, C. J. P.: *Roof Bosses in Medieval Churches*, Cambridge, England, 1948.

CAWLEY, A. C., ed.: 'The Sykes Manuscript of the York Scriveners' Play,' *Leeds Studies in English and Kindred Languages*, Nos. 7 and 8, 45–80 (1952); *The Wakefield Pageants in the Towneley Cycle*, Manchester, 1958; *Everyman*, Manchester, 1961.

CAWLEY, A. C., and STEVENS, M., eds.: *The Towneley Cycle: A Facsimile of Huntington MS HM 1*, Leeds, 1976.

CHAMBERS, E. K.: *The Mediaeval Stage*, 2 vols., Oxford, 1903; *English Literature at the Close of the Middle Ages*, Oxford, 1945, 1947.

CLARK, W. S.: *The Early Irish Stage*, Oxford, 1955.

COGHILL, N.: 'The Case for University Drama,' *The Universities Quarterly*, i. 159–65 (1948).

CORMICAN, L. A.: 'Morality Tradition and the Interludes,' in *The Age of Chaucer* (ed. B. Ford), Penguin Books, 1954.

COSBEY, R. C.: 'The Mak Story and its Folklore Analogues,' *Speculum*, xx. 310–17 (1945).

CRAIG, H., ed.: *Two Coventry Corpus Christi Plays*, Early English Text Society, Extra Series, 87 (1902, 1957); *English Religious Drama of the Middle Ages*, Oxford, 1955.

DAVIES, R. T., ed.: *The Corpus Christi Play of the English Middle Ages*, London, 1972.

DAVIS, N., ed.: *Non-Cycle Plays and Fragments*, Early English Text Society, Supplementary Text, I (1970); ed.: *Paston Letters and Papers of the Fifteenth Century*, Part II, Oxford, 1976.

DEIMLING, H., and Dr MATTHEWS, eds.: *The Chester Plays*, Early English Text Society, Extra Series, 62 and 115 (1892, 1916).

DICKINS, B., and WILSON, R. M., eds.: *Early Middle English Texts*, Bowes and Bowes, Cambridge, England, 1951.

DILLER, H.-J.: *Redeformen des englischen Misterienspiels*, Munich, 1973.

DORRELL, MARGARET: 'Performance in Procession: A Medieval Stage for the York Corpus Christi Play,' *Leeds Studies in English*, new series, vi. 77–111 (1972).

EDWARDS, F.: *Ritual and Drama: The Mediaeval Theatre*, Guildford and London, 1976.

ELIOT, T. S.: *Religious Drama: Medieval and Modern*, New York, 1954.

ELLIOTT, J. R.: 'Medieval Rounds and Wooden O's: The Medieval Heritage of the Elizabethan Theatre,' in *Medieval Drama* (ed. N. Denny), Stratford-upon-Avon Studies 16, London, 1973.

ENGLAND, G., and POLLARD, A. W., eds.: *The Towneley Plays*, Early English Text Society, Extra Series, 71 (1897, 1952).

FARNHAM, W.: *The Medieval Heritage of Elizabethan Tragedy*, Blackwell, Oxford, 1956.

FIFIELD, MERLE: *The Rhetoric of Free Will: The Five-action Structure of the English Morality Play*, Leeds, 1974.

FRAMPTON, M. G.: 'The Date of the Flourishing of the "Wakefield Master",' *Publications of the Modern Language Association of America*, 1. 631–60 (1935).

FRANK, G.: *The Medieval French Drama*, Oxford, 1954.

FRY, T.: 'The Unity of the *Ludus Coventriae*,' *Studies in Philology*, xlviii. 527–70 (1951).

FURNIVALL, F. J., ed.: *The Digby Plays*, Early English Text Society, Extra Series, 70 (1896, 1930).

FURNIVALL, F. J., and POLLARD, A. W., eds.: *The Macro Plays*, Early English Text Society, Extra Series, 91 (1904, 1924); ed. Mark Eccles, Early English Text Society, 262 (1969).

GARDINER, H. C.: *Mysteries' End: An Investigation of the Last Days of the Medieval Religious Stage*, New Haven, 1946.

GARDNER, J.: *The Construction of the Wakefield Cycle*, Carbondale and Edwardsville, 1974.

GASCOIGNE, B.: *World Theatre: An Illustrated History*, London, 1971.

GAYLEY, C. M.: *Plays of Our Forefathers*, New York, 1907

GREG, W. W., ed.: *Everyman*, in *Materialien zur Kunde des älteren englischen Dramas*, iv, xxiv, xxviii, Louvain, 1904, 1909, 1910; 'Bibliographical and Textual Problems of the English Miracle Cycles,' *The Library*, 3rd series, v. 1, 168, 280, 365 (1914).

GREG, W. W., and SALTER, F. M., eds.: *The Trial and Flagellation with Other Studies in the Chester Cycle*, Malone Society, Oxford, 1935.

HALLIDAY, F. E., ed.: *The Legend of the Rood*, London, 1955.

HAPPÉ, P., ed.: *English Mystery Plays: A Selection*, Penguin Books, 1975.

HARBAGE, A., and SCHOENBAUM, S.: *Annals of English Drama 975–1700*, London, 1964.

HARDISON, O. B., Jr.: *Christian Rite and Christian Drama in the Middle Ages*, Baltimore, 1965.

HARRIS, M., trans.: *The Cornish Ordinalia: A Medieval Dramatic Trilogy*, Washington, D.C., 1969.

HILDBURGH, W. L.: 'English Alabaster Carvings as Records of Medieval Religious Drama,' *Archaeologia*, xciii. 51–101 (1949).

HOSLEY, R.: 'Three Kinds of Outdoor Theatre before Shakespeare,' *Theatre Survey*, xii. 1–33 (1971).

HUSSEY, M., ed.: *The Chester Mystery Plays: Sixteen Pageant Plays from the Chester Craft Cycle*, London, 1957.

JAMES, E. O.: *Christian Myth and Ritual*, London, 1933.

JAMES, M. R.: *The Apocryphal New Testament*, Oxford, 1924.

KAHRL, S. J.: *Traditions of Medieval English Drama*, London, 1974; ed.: *Collections VIII, Records of Plays and Players in Lincolnshire 1300–1585*, Malone Society, Oxford, 1974.

KINGHORN, A. M.: *Mediaeval Drama*, London, 1968.

KOLVE, V. A.: *The Play Called Corpus Christi*, London, 1966.
LEACH, A. F.: 'Some English Plays and Players, 1220–1548,' in *An English Miscellany presented to Dr Furnivall*, Oxford, 1901.
LONGSWORTH, R.: *The Cornish Ordinalia: Religion and Dramaturgy*, Cambridge, Mass., 1967.
LOOMIS, R. S., and COHEN, G.: 'Were there Theatres in the Twelfth and Thirteenth Centuries?' *Speculum*, xx. 92–8 (1945).
LUMIANSKY, R. M., and MILLS, D., eds.: *The Chester Mystery Cycle: A Facsimile of MS Bodley 175*, Leeds, 1973; *The Chester Mystery Cycle*, Early English Text Society, S.S.3 (1974).
MACKENZIE, W. R.: *The English Moralities from the Point of View of Allegory*, Boston and London, 1914.
McNEIR, W. F.: 'The Corpus Christi Passion Plays as Dramatic Art,' *Studies in Philology*, xlviii. 601–28 (1951).
MÂLE, E.: *L'Art religieux de la fin du moyen âge en France*, 3rd ed., Paris, 1925.
MANLY, J. M., ed.: *Specimens of the Pre-Shaksperean Drama*, 2 vols., Boston, 1897, 1903
MANTZIUS, K.: *A History of Theatrical Art in Ancient and Modern Times*, 6 vols., London, 1903–21.
MILL, A. J.: *Mediaeval Plays in Scotland*, St Andrews University Publications, xxiv (1927); 'Noah's Wife Again,' *Publications of the Modern Language Association of America*, lxi. 613–26 (1941).
NAGLER, A. M.: *The Medieval Religious Stage: Shapes and Phantoms*, New Haven and London, 1976.
NICOLL, A.: *The Development of the Theatre*, London, 1927, 1966.
NORRIS, E., ed.: *The Ancient Cornish Drama*, 2 vols., Oxford, 1859.
OWST, G. R.: *Literature and Pulpit in Medieval England*, Cambridge, England, 1933; 2nd ed., Blackwell, Oxford, 1961.
PASCAL, R.: 'On the Origins of the Liturgical Drama of the Middle Ages,' *Modern Language Review*, xxxvi. 369–87 (1941).
PATRIDES, C. A.: *The Grand Design of God: The literary form of the Christian view of history*, London, 1972.
PROSSER, ELEANOR: *Drama and Religion in the English Mystery Plays*, Stanford, 1961.
PURVIS, J. S.: *From Minster to Market Place*, York, 1969.
RAINE, A., ed.: *York Civic Records*, i, Yorkshire Archaeological Society, Record Series, 98 (1938).
ROSE, M., ed.: *The Wakefield Mystery Plays*, London, 1961.
ROSSITER, A. P.: *English Drama from Early Times to the Elizabethans*, London, 1950.
ROSTON, M.: *Biblical Drama in England*, London, 1968.
RUSHFORTH, G. McN.: *Medieval Christian Imagery*, Oxford, 1936.
SALTER, F. M.: *Mediaeval Drama in Chester*, Toronto, 1955.
SCHAPIRO, M.: 'Cain's Jaw-bone that did the First Murder,' *Art Bulletin*, xxiv. 205 (1942).
SELLERS, M., ed.; *York Memorandum Book*, i, Surtees Society, 120 (1912).
SEVERS, J. BURKE: 'The Relationship between the Brome and Chester Plays of *Abraham and Isaac*,' *Modern Philology*, xlii. 137–51 (1945).

SHARP, THOMAS: *A Dissertation on the Pageants or Dramatic Mysteries Anciently performed at Coventry, by the Trading Companies of that City*, Coventry, 1825; repr. EP Publishing Ltd, 1973.

SMART, W. K.: '*Mankind* and the Mumming Plays,' *Modern Language Notes*, xxxii. 21–5 (1917).

SMITH, L. TOULMIN, ed.: *York Plays*, Oxford, 1885.

SMOLDON, W. L.: 'Liturgical Drama,' chap. vi in *Early Medieval Music up to 1300* (ed. Dom Anselm Hughes), The New Oxford History of Music, ii, Oxford, 1955.

SOUTHERN, R.: *The Medieval Theatre in the Round: A Study of the Staging of 'The Castle of Perseverance' and Related Matters*, London, 1957; *The Seven Ages of the Theatre*, London, 1962; 2nd ed., 1964.

SPEIRS, J.: *Medieval English Poetry: The Non-Chaucerian Tradition*, London, 1957; 'The Mystery Cycle: Some Towneley Cycle Plays,' *Scrutiny*, xviii. 86–117, 246–65 (1951, 1952).

STEVENS, M.: 'The Theatre of the World: A Study in Medieval Dramatic Form,' *Chaucer Review*, vii. 234–49 (1973).

STRATMAN, C. J.: *Bibliography of Medieval Drama*, 2 vols., 2nd ed., New York, 1972.

THOMAS, R. G., ed.: *Ten Miracle Plays*, York Medieval Texts, London, 1966.

TIDDY, R. J. E.: *The Mummers' Play*, Oxford, 1923.

TRISTRAM, E. W.: *English Medieval Wall Painting: The Twelfth and Thirteenth Centuries*, 3 vols., Oxford, 1944–50.

VOCHT, H. DE: *Everyman: A Comparative Study of Texts and Sources*, Materials for the Study of Old English Drama, xx, Louvain, 1947.

WALKER, J. W.: *Wakefield: Its History and People*, 2 vols., 2nd ed., Wakefield, 1939.

WARNER, G., ed.: *Queen Mary's Psalter*, London, 1912.

WATT, H. A.: 'The Dramatic Unity of the *Secunda Pastorum*,' in *Essays and Studies in Honor of Carleton Brown*, New York, 1940.

WELFORD, R.: *History of Newcastle and Gateshead*, 3 vols., London, 1884–7.

WICKHAM, G.: *Early English Stages 1300 to 1660*, i, 1300–1576, London, 1959; *The Medieval Theatre*, London, 1974.

WILLIAMS, A.: *The Characterization of Pilate in the Towneley Plays*, East Lansing, 1950; *The Drama of Medieval England*, East Lansing, 1961.

WILLIAMS, R.: *Drama in Performance*, London, 1954.

WILSON, F. P.: *The English Drama 1485–1585*, Oxford, 1969.

WILSON, R. M.: *Early Middle English Literature*, London, 1939; *The Lost Literature of Medieval England*, London, 1952.

WOOLF, ROSEMARY: *The English Mystery Plays*, London, 1972.

YOUNG, K.: *The Drama of the Medieval Church*, 2 vols., Oxford, 1933.

ZANDVOORT, R. W.: '*Everyman—Elckerlijc*,' in *Collected Papers*, Groningen, 1954.

CONTENTS

THE CREATION,
AND THE FALL OF LUCIFER

The York cycle, like all other Corpus Christi cycles, surveys the spiritual history of mankind 'From the creation to the general doom.' The first five pageants of the York cycle are concerned with the different events of the Creation, culminating in the temptation and fall of man. The same events are more briefly dramatized in the other English cycles and in the Cornish plays.

The fall of Lucifer, which forms part of the opening pageant of all the English cycles, is a non-biblical theme of great antiquity: already well established in Old English literature, it goes back to commentaries on Genesis and to exegetical writings of the Church Fathers concerned with the six days of creation.

This pageant of the barkers (i.e. tanners) of York is attributed to an author known as the 'York metrist,' who uses both iambic (as in the *Resurrection*) and alliterative verse. The *Creation* is written in alliterative verse, in which the line is divided by a medial pause, with two stressed syllables (emphasized by alliteration) in each half-line. Such verse is not a decadent kind of iambic metre, but a development of the alliterative long-line of Old English poetry. The playwright shows considerable skill in controlling his metre and in grouping his lines into eight-line stanzas with the rhyme-sequence *ababcddc* and occasionally *ababcccc*.

The forty-eight pageants of the York cycle are preserved in a fifteenth-century manuscript (British Museum MS. Additional 35290), which was once the property of the York municipal authorities (see Introduction, p. xi). The whole cycle has been edited by L. Toulmin Smith.

CHARACTERS

GOD

ANGEL SERAPHIM   LUCIFER

ANGEL CHERUBIM   SECOND ANGEL
                              (*afterwards* SECOND DEVIL)

THE CREATION,
AND THE FALL OF LUCIFER

[Scene I. *Heaven*]

God. *I am Alpha and Omega, the life, the way, the truth, the*
the first and the last.

I am gracious and great, God without beginning;
I am maker unmade, all might is in me;
I am life and way unto wealth-winning;
I am foremost and first, as I bid shall it be.
5   On blessing my blee shall be blending,
And hielding from harm to be hiding,
My body in bliss ay abiding,
Unending without any ending.

Since I am maker unmade, and most so of might,
10   And ay shall be endless, and nought is but I,
Unto my dignity dear shall duly be dight   *made*
A place full of plenty to my pleasing at ply;
And therewith also will I have wrought
Many divers doings bedene,
15   Which work shall meekly contain,   *continue*
And all shall be made even of nought.

But only the worthly work of my will
In my spirit shall inspire the might of me;
And in the first, faithly my thoughts to fulfil,   *faithfully*
20   Bainly in my blessing I bid at here be
A bliss all-bielding about me;

3 *wealth-winning*, attainment of felicity.
5–6 My countenance shall be immanent in my blessing, and where it
inclines shall protect from harm.
12 A place of plenty to mould to my liking.
14 Many different things forthwith.
17–18 But my might shall inspire with my spirit only the worthy work
of my will.
20–1 At once with my blessing I bid an all-protecting bliss to be here
about me.

3

In the which bliss I bid at be here   *to*
Nine orders of angels full clear,   *bright*
In lofing ay-lasting at lout me.   *praise; reverence*

Then the angels sing: Te Deum laudamus.

25 Here underneath me now an isle I neven,   *name*
     Which isle shall be earth.   Now all be at once:
     Earth, wholly, and hell; this highest be heaven,
     And that wealth shall wield shall won in these
       wones.
     This grant I you, ministers mine,   *servants*
30 To-whiles ye are stable in thought;   *while*
     And also to them that are nought
     Be put to my prison at pine.

[*To Lucifer:*

     Of all the mights I have made most next after me, *powers*
     I make thee as master and mirror of my might;
35 I bield thee here bainly, in bliss for to be, *protect; at once*
     I name thee for Lucifer, as bearer of light.
     Nothing here shall thee be dering: *harming*
     In this bliss shall be your bielding,   *protection*
     And have all wealth in your wielding,   *possession*
40 Ay whiles ye are buxomly bearing.

Then the angels sing: Holy, holy, holy, Lord God of hosts.

Seraphim.   Ah, merciful maker, full mickle is thy might,
     That all this work at a word worthily has wrought;
     Ay lofed be that lovely Lord of his light,
     That us thus mighty has made, that now were
      right nought.
45 In bliss for to bide, in his blessing
     Ay-lasting, in lof let us lout him,   *praise*
     At bield us thus bainly about him,   *for protecting*
     Of mirth nevermore to have missing.   *joy; lack*

28 And those who shall enjoy felicity shall live in this dwelling.
31-2 And also [I promise] those who are worthless that they shall be put
in my prison to suffer torment.
40 As long as you behave obediently.
43 May that loving Lord be for ever praised for his radiance.

Lucifer. All the mirth that is made is marked   *fashioned*
     in me!
50 The beams of my brighthead are burning so   *brightness*
     bright,
     And I so seemly in sight myself now I see,
     For like a lord am I left to lend in this light.   *dwell*
     More fairer by far than my feres,   *companions*
     In me is no point that may pair;   *deteriorate*
55 I feel me featous and fair,   *myself well-formed*
     My power is passing my peers.   *surpassing*

Cherubim. Lord, with a lasting lof we lof thee alone,
     Thou mightful maker that marked us and made us,   *mighty*
     And wrought us thus worthily to won in this wone,
60 There never feeling of filth may foul us nor fade us.
     All bliss is here bielding about us: *dwelling*
     To-whiles we are stable in thought
     In the worship of him that us wrought,
     Of dere never thar us more doubt us.

65 *Luc.* Oh, what I am featous and figured full fit!
     The form of all fairhead upon me is fest;
     All wealth in my wield is, I wot by my wit,   *possession*
     The beams of my brighthead are bigged with the
     best,
     My showing is shimmering and shining.   *appearance*
70 So bigly to bliss am I brought,   *firmly*
     Me needs for to noy me right nought;
     Here shall never pain me be pining.   *tormenting*

Seraph. With all the wit at we wield we worship   *that*
     thy will,
     Thou glorious God that art ground of all grace;
75 Ay with steadfast steven let us stand still,   *voice*
     Lord, to be fed with the food of thy fair face.

51 And now I see myself so handsome to look at.
60 Where never impure thought may defile nor corrupt us.
64 We need never be afraid of harm.
65–6 Oh, how handsome I am and fitly shaped! The form of all
beauty is fixed in me.
68 Among the best made.
71 I need not trouble myself at all.

In life that is leally ay-lasting,   *truly*
Thy dole, Lord, art ay daintily dealing,
And whoso that food may be feeling—   *tasting*
80   To see thy fair face—is not fasting.

    Luc. Oh certes, what I am worthily wrought with
        worship, iwis!
For in a glorious glee my glittering it gleams.
I am so mightily made my mirth may not miss;   *fail*
Ay shall I bide in this bliss through brightness of
    beams.
85   Me needs not of noy for to neven;
All wealth in my wield have I wielding;
Above yet shall I be bielding,
On height in the highest of heaven.   *high*

There shall I set myself, full seemly to sight,
90   To receive my reverence through right of renown;
I shall be like unto him that is highest on height.
Oh, what I am dearworth and deft!—
    Oh, deuce! all goes down:

               [The bad angels fall from heaven.

My might and my main are all marrand;   *passing away*
Help, fellows, in faith I am falland!   *falling*
95 *2 Angel.* From heaven are we hielding on all hand;
To woe are we wending, I warrant.

[SCENE II. *Hell*]

    Luc. Out, out, harrow! helpless, slike hot at is here;
This is a dungeon of dole that I am to   *misery; put into*
    dight.
Where is my kind become, so comely and clear?
100   Now am I loathest, alas, that ere was light.

78 Thy gift, Lord, thou art ever generously bestowing.
81–2 In truth, how worthily and honourably made I am, to be sure!
For my glittering [shape] gleams in glorious joy.
85–6 I need not talk of harm; I have all felicity at my command.
92 How noble and clever I am!
95 Falling on all sides.
97 Help, help! helpless [am I], for the heat here is so great.
99 What has become of my nature.

My brightness is blackest and blue now;
My bale is ay beeting and burning:
That gars me go gowling and grinning.
Out, ay welaway!   I well enough in woe now.   *alas; boil*

105 2 *Devil.*   Out, out!   I go wood for woe, my wit is   *mad*
    all went now;   *gone*
All our food is but filth we find us beforn.   *before*
We that were bielded in bliss, in bale are we brent now;   *burnt*
Out on thee, Lucifer, lurdan! our light hast thou lorn.
Thy deeds to this dole now have dight us,
110 To spill us thou wast our speeder;   *destroy; helper*
For thou wast our light and our leader,
The highest of heaven had thou hight us.   *promised*

   Luc.   Welaway! woe is me now—now is it worse
    than it was.
Unthrivingly threap ye; I said but a thought.
115 2 *Dev.*   We! lurdan, thou lost us.   *ruined*
Luc.   Ye lie, out, alas!
I wist not this woe should be wrought.   *knew*
Out on you, lurdans! ye smore me in smoke.   *smother*
2 *Dev.*   This woe hast thou wrought us.
Luc.   Ye lie, ye lie!
2 *Dev.*   Thou liest, and that shalt thou buy;   *pay for*
120 We! lurdan, have at you, let loke!

[SCENE III.   *Heaven*]

   Cherub.   Ah, Lord, lofed be thy name that us this
    light lent!   *granted*
Since Lucifer our leader is lighted so low,   *descended*
For his unbuxomness in bale to be brent—   *disobedience*
Thy righteousness to reward on row
125 Ilk work after his wrought—

102-3 My torment is ever kindling and burning: that makes me go
howling and snarling.
108 Rascal! you have made us lose our radiance.
114 You chide in vain; I was only thinking aloud.
115 *We!*, an exclamation of grief.
120 Watch me get at you!
124-5 Thy righteousness duly rewarding each action according to its
deserts.

Through grace of thy merciful might
The cause I see it in sight
Wherefore to bale he is brought.

God. Those fools for their fairhead in fantasies fell,
130   And made moan of might that marked them   *complained*
        and made them;
Forthy after their works were, in woe shall they well,
For some are fallen into filth that evermore shall
        fade them,   *corrupt*
And never shall have grace to grith   *make their peace*
        them.
So passing of power they thought them,
135   They would not me worship that wrought them;
Forthy shall my wrath ever go with them.

And all that me worship shall won here, iwis;   *live*
Forthy more forth of my work, work now I will.
Since then their might is formarred that meant all
        amiss,
140   Even to my own figure, this bliss to fulfil,
Mankind of mould will I make;   *earth*
But first will I form him before
All thing that shall him restore,   *refresh*
To which that his talents will take.

145   And in my first making to muster my might,   *show*
Since earth is vain and void and mirkness imell,
I bid in my blessing ye angels give light
To the earth, for it faded when the fiends fell.
In hell shall never mirkness be missing;
150   The mirkness, thus name I for night;
The day, that call I this light:
My after-works shall they be wissing.   *guiding*

129 Those fools because of their beauty fell into vain imaginings.
131 Therefore according as their actions were.
138 Therefore I will now go on and do more of my work.
139–40 Since their power is utterly destroyed who meant nothing but
ill, even in my own image, to occupy this place of bliss (i.e. the place left
vacant by the fallen angels).
142 But first before him I will form.
144 To which his desires will incline.
146 Since earth is vacant and void and in the midst of darkness.

And now in my blessing I twin them in two,   *separate*
The night even from the day, so that they meet never,
155   But either in a kind course their gates for to go.
Both the night and the day, do duly your dever: *duty*
To all I shall work be ye wissing.
This day's work is done ilka deal,   *every part*
And all this work likes me right well,   *pleases*
160   And bainly I give it my blessing.

155 But each to go their ways according to the course of nature.

THE CREATION OF ADAM AND EVE

The dramatization of the story of Adam and Eve has a long history. As early as the twelfth century there is an Anglo-Norman play of Adam (*Jeu d'Adam*), in which Latin is mingled with the vernacular. And even after the extinction of the medieval religious stage in the last decades of the sixteenth century the Adam pageant was still preserved in puppet shows; it is to these that Milton refers in the *Areopagitica* (1644), when he writes of 'a mere artificial Adam, such an Adam as he is in the motions.'

All the Corpus Christi playwrights dramatized this subject, and the Norwich Grocers' Company acted a pageant on the *Creation of Eve and Expulsion from Eden*. (For some of the properties used in the Norwich play see Introduction, p. xiii.)

The cardmakers, to whom the third York pageant belonged, were a guild of craftsmen who made cards for combing wool. They are one of several representatives of the woollen industry associated with pageants in the York cycle: among them are the fullers, who acted the fourth pageant on the induction of Adam and Eve into paradise. Such guilds bear witness to the fact that York was still the centre of the Yorkshire cloth trade in the fifteenth century, although West Riding towns like Wakefield and Halifax were becoming increasingly important.

CHARACTERS

GOD

ADAM   EVE

THE CREATION OF ADAM AND EVE

[SCENE. *The World*]

God. In heaven and earth duly bedene
    Of five days' work, even unto the end,
    I have completed by courses clean;
    Methinketh the space of them well spent.

5   In heaven are angels fair and bright,
    Stars and planets their courses to go;
    The moon serves unto the night,
    The sun to light the day also.

    In earth are trees and grass to spring;
10   Beasts and fowls both great and small,   *birds*
    Fishes in flood, all other thing,
    Thrive and have my blessing, all.

    This work is wrought now at my will,
    But yet can I here no beast see
15   That accords by kindly skill,
    And for my work might worship me.

    For perfect work ne were there none
    But aught were made that might it yeme;
    For lof made I this world alone,   *praise*
20   Therefore my lof shall in it seem.   *be manifest*

    To keep this world, both more and less,   *look after*
    A skilful beast then will I make   *rational*
    After my shape and my likeness,
    The which shall worship to me take.   *do*

1–3 In heaven and earth I have duly completed the work of five days in
perfect stages, even to the end.
15 That gives assent by natural reason.
17–18 For there would be no perfect work unless something were made
that could have charge of it.

25 Of the simplest part of earth that is here
    I shall make man, and for this skill: *reason*
    For to abate his haughty cheer,   *temper*
    Both his great pride and other ill;

    And also for to have in mind
30 How simple he is at his making,
    For as feeble I shall him find
    When he is dead, at his ending.

    For this reason and skill alone,
    I shall make man like unto me.
35 Rise up, thou earth, in blood and bone,
    In shape of man, I command thee!

    A female shalt thou have to fere;   *as a mate*
    Her shall I make of thy left rib,
    Alone so shalt thou not be here,
40 Without faithful friend and sib.   *relation*

    Take now here the ghost of life,   *spirit*
    And receive both your souls of me;
    This female take thou to thy wife:
    Adam and Eve your names shall be.

45 *Adam.* Ah, Lord, full mickle is thy might,   *great*
    And that is seen in ilka side;   *every*
    For now is here a joyful sight,
    To see this world so long and wide.

    Many diverse things now here is,
50 Of beasts and fowls, both wild and tame;
    Yet is none made to thy likeness
    But we alone.   Ah, lofed be thy name!   *praised*

    Eve.   To such a Lord in all degree
    Be evermore lasting lofing,   *praise*
55 That to us such a dignity
    Has given before all other thing.   *above*

And selcouth things may we see here,   *wondrous*
Of this ilk world so long and broad,   *same*
With beasts and fowls so many and sere;   *various*
60 Blessed be he that has us made!

Adam.   Ah, blessed Lord, now at thy will
Since we are wrought, vouchsafe to tell
And also say us two until,   *unto*
What we shall do and where to dwell.

65 *God.*   For this skill made I you this day—
My name to worship aywhere.   *everywhere*
Love me forthy and lof me ay   *therefore*
For my making; I ask no more.

Both wise and witty shalt thou be,   *intelligent*
70 As man that I have made of nought;
Lordship on earth then grant I thee,
All thing to serve thee that is wrought.

In paradise shall ye sam won;   *together dwell*
Of earthly thing get ye no need.
75 Ill and good both shall ye con;
I shall you learn your life to lead.   *teach*

Adam.   Ah, Lord since we shall do no thing
But lof thee for thy great goodness,
We shall obey to thy bidding,
80 And fulfil it both more and less.   *entirely*

Eve.   His sign since he has on us set
Before all other thing, certain,   *certainly*
Him for to lof we shall not let,   *cease*
And worship him with might and main.

85 *God.*   At heaven and earth first I began,
And six days wrought ere I would rest;
My work is ended now at man:
All likes me well, but this the best.   *pleases*

74–5 You shall not lack any earthly thing. You shall know [the
difference between] evil and good.

My blessing have they ever and ay.
90 The seventh day shall my resting be;
Thus will I cease, soothly to say,
Of my doing in this degree.

To bliss I shall you bring;
Come forth, ye two, with me.
95 Ye shall live in liking;   *delight*
My blessing with you be.   Amen.

92 From my work at this stage.

The York Pageant of the Coopers

THE FALL OF MAN

The York pageant on the *Fall of Man* is the fifth in the cycle. The craft responsible for producing this pageant was the guild of coopers (i.e. makers of casks and buckets). Roger Burton, the town clerk of York, in a list of the York pageants drawn up in 1415, summarizes the story as follows: 'Adam and Eve and the tree between them, a serpent deceiving them with apples; God speaking to them and cursing the serpent, and an angel with a sword driving them from Paradise' (translated from Burton's Latin; see L. Toulmin Smith, p. xx).

The stanza used in this pageant has eleven lines rhyming *ababcbcdcdc*, with a predominantly iambic rhythm and with stresses varying between four in the longest lines and one or two in the shortest.

CHARACTERS

GOD

SATAN   ADAM

EVE   ANGEL

THE FALL OF MAN

[Scene I. *Hell*]

Satan.   For woe my wit is in a were!   *confusion*
    That moves me mickle in my mind:
    The Godhead that I saw so clear,
    And perceived that he should take kind
5   Of a degree
    That he had wrought, and I disdained that angel
      kind
    Should it not be.
    And we were fair and bright,
    Therefore me thought that he
10 The kind of us take might,
    And thereat disdained me.

    The kind of man he thought to take,   *nature*
    And thereat had I great envy;
    But he has made to him a make,
15 And hard to her I will me hie   *quickly*
    That ready way,
    That purpose proof to put it by,
    And fand to pick from him that prey.
    My travail were well set
20 Might I him so betray,
    His liking for to let;
    And soon I shall essay.

2–7 This greatly disturbs my mind: that I saw the Godhead so clearly, and perceived that He would take the nature of an order [of beings] He had created, and I was angry that it would not be an angelic nature.

9–11 Therefore I thought that He might take our nature, and I was angry [because He did not do so].

14 But He has made a mate for him (i.e. Adam).

17–21 To set aside that firm purpose, and try to steal from him that prey (i.e. Eve). My efforts would be well spent if I could so betray him as to spoil his pleasure.

[SCENE II. *Paradise*]

In a worm's likeness will I wend, *serpent's*
And fand to feign a loud leasing.
25 Eve! Eve!
Eve.　　　　Who is there?
Sat.　　　　　　　I, a friend;
And for thy good is the coming
I hither sought.
Of all the fruit that ye see hang
In Paradise, why eat ye nought?
30 *Eve.*　We may of them ilkane
Take all that us good thought,
Save a tree out is ta'en,
Would do harm to nigh it aught.

Sat.　And why *that* tree—that would I wit— *know*
35　Any more than all other by? *nearby*
Eve.　For our Lord God forbids us it, *because*
The fruit thereof, Adam nor I,
To nigh it near;　. *go near it*
And if we did, we both should die,
40　He said, and cease our solace sere.
Sat.　Yea, Eve, to me take tent; *pay attention*
Take heed, and thou shalt hear
What that the matter meant
He moved on that manner.

45　To eat thereof he you defend,
I know it well; this was his skill,
Because he would none other kenned
These great virtues that long theretill.
For wilt thou see,

24 And try to concoct a flagrant lie.
26–7 It is for your good I have come here to see you.
30–3 We may of each of them take all we please, with the exception of one tree, to approach which would harm us.
40 And cease to enjoy our various delights.
43–4 What He meant by speaking in that way.
45–8 He forbade you to eat thereof, I know it well; this was His reason, that He wished no one else should know the great virtues which belong thereto.

50 Who eats the fruit, of good and ill
    Shall have knowing as well as he.   *knowledge*
    Eve. Why, what kin thing art thou   *kind of*
    That tells this tale to me?
    Sat. A worm, that woteth well how   *knows*
55 That ye may worshipped be.   *honoured*

    Eve. What worship should we win thereby?
    To eat thereof us needeth it nought;
    We have lordship to make mastery
    Of all thing that in earth is wrought.   *over*
60 *Sat.* Woman, do way!   *enough!*
    To greater state ye may be brought,
    And ye will do as I shall say.   *if*
    Eve. To do is us full loath
    That should our God mispay.   *displease*
65 *Sat.* Nay, certes, it is no wothe: *truly; danger*
    Eat it safely ye may.

    For peril right none therein lies,
    But worship and a great winning;   *advantage*
    For right as God ye shall be wise,
70 And peer to him in all kin thing:
    Ay, gods shall ye be,
    Of ill and good to have knowing,
    For to be as wise as he.
    Eve. Is this sooth that thou says?
75 *Sat.* Yea, why trowest thou not me?   *believe*
    I would by no kins ways   *by no means*
    Tell nought but truth to thee.

    Eve. Then will I to thy teaching trust,
    And fang this fruit unto our food.   *take*
               And then she must take the apple.
80 *Sat.* Bite on boldly, be not abashed,   *afraid*
    And bear Adam to amend his mood
    And eke his bliss.   *Then Satan retires.*
    Eve. Adam, have here of fruit full good.

    58 We have authority to exercise control.
    81–2 And persuade Adam to be of better cheer and add to his bliss.

Adam.   Alas, woman, why took'st thou this?
85   Our Lord commanded us both
        To tent the tree of his.   *give heed to*
        Thy work will make him wroth:
        Alas, thou hast done amiss!

        Eve.   Nay, Adam, grieve thee not at it,
90   And I shall say thee reason why:
        A worm has done me for to wit   *caused*
        We shall be as gods, thou and I,
        If that we eat
        Here of this tree.   Adam, forthy   *therefore*
95   Let not that worship for to get,
        For we shall be as wise
        As God that is so great,
        And as mickle of price;   *worth*
        Forthy eat of this meat.   *food*

100 *Adam.*   To eat it would I not eschew,
        Might I me sure in thy saying.
        Eve.   Bite on boldly, for it is true:
        We shall be gods and know all thing.
        Adam.   To win that name,
105   I shall it taste at thy teaching.   *He takes and eats.*
        Alas, what have I done? for shame!
        Ill counsel, woe worth thee!   *befall*
        Ah, Eve, thou art to blame;
        To this enticed thou me;
110   Me shames with my lichame,

        For I am naked, as methink.
        Eve.   Alas, Adam, right so am I.
        Adam.   And for sorrow sere why ne might we sink?
        For we have grieved God Almighty
115   That made me man,
        Broken his bidding bitterly: *grievously*
        Alas, that ever we it began!

        95 Do not fail to get that honour.
        101 If I could be sure of the truth of what you are saying.
        110 I am ashamed of my body.
        113 Why may we not sink under the weight of our several sorrows?

This work, Eve, hast thou wrought,
And made this bad bargain.
120 *Eve.*   Nay, Adam, wite me nought.   *blame*
Adam.   Do way, lief Eve! whom then?   *dear*

Eve.   The worm to wite well worthy were;
With tales untrue he me betrayed.
Adam.   Alas, that I let at thy lore,
125 Or trowed the trifles that thou me said.   *lies*
So may I bid,
For I may ban that bitter braid,
And dreary deed that I it did.
Our shape for dole me deaves,
130 Wherewith they shall be hid.
Eve.   Let us take these fig-leaves,
Since it is thus betid.   *happened*

Adam.   Right as thou say'st so shall it be,
For we are naked and all bare.
135 Full wonder fain I would hide me
From my Lord's sight, and I wist where,
Where I ne rought.
God.   Adam! Adam!
Adam.   Lord?
God.   Where art thou? yare!   *quickly*
Adam.   I hear thee, Lord, and see thee nought.
140 *God.*   Say, whereon is it long?
This work why hast thou wrought?
Adam.   Lord, Eve gart me to do wrong,   *caused*
And to that breach me brought.   *breach of duty*

God.   Say, Eve, why hast thou gart thy make   *mate*
145 Eat fruit I bade thee should hang still,   *always*
And commanded none of it to take?

124 Alas, that I listened to your advice.
126–30 So must I pray [for God's mercy], for I may well curse that
cruel trick and the dire deed I have done. Our bodies bewilder me with
grief, [and I do not know] what to hide them with.
135–7 I would most gladly hide myself from my Lord's sight where I
should have nothing to fear, if only I knew where.
140 Tell me, what is the reason for it?

    Eve.   A worm, Lord, enticed me theretill;   *thereto*
    So welaway   *alas*
    That ever I did that deed so dill!   *foolish*
150 *God.*   Ah, wicked worm, woe worth thee ay!
    For thou on this manner
    Hast made them such affray,
    My malison have thou here   *curse*
    With all the might I may.

155   And on thy womb then shalt thou glide,   *belly*
    And be ay full of enmity
    To all mankind on ilka side;   *every*
    And earth it shall thy sustenance be
    To eat and drink.
160   Adam and Eve, also, ye
    In earth then shall ye sweat and swink,   *toil*
    And travail for your food.   *labour*
    Adam.   Alas, why ne might we sink?
    We that have all world's good,
165   Full derfly may us think.

    God.   Now Cherubim, mine angel bright,
    To middle-earth tite go drive these two.   *quickly*
    Angel.   All ready, Lord, as it is right,
    Since thy will is that it be so,
170   And thy liking.
    Adam and Eve, do you two go,
    For here may ye make no dwelling.
    Go ye forth fast to fare;
    Of sorrow may ye sing.
175 *Adam.*   Alas, for sorrow and care
    Our hands may we wring!

    151–2 Because you have disturbed them in this way.
    165 Most grievous it may seem to us, i.e. we shall have ample cause
for grief.
    167 *middle-earth*, i.e. the world outside Paradise.
    173 Go forth and go quickly.

THE N. TOWN CYCLE

CAIN AND ABEL

The N. town cycle, to which this pageant belongs, was once believed to be the Corpus Christi play of Coventry, and it is still often referred to as the *Ludus Coventriae*. In fact, it has nothing to do with Coventry, from which two pageants only have survived (see p. 69). The description 'N. town cycle' is taken from the Banns prefixed to the pageants, in which the announcement is made that a performance will be given on a following Sunday at 6 a.m. 'in N. town' (where N. may simply stand for *Nomen*, as it does in the Prayer Book). Possibly the N. town play was acted by touring players; in any case there is nothing to associate it with a particular town or with trade guilds.

The biblical story of Cain and Abel, as dramatized in this pageant and in the corresponding pageant of the other cycles, has been strongly influenced by medieval legend. Thus the legends of Cain commonly made him offer God his worst produce, and not simply 'of the fruit of the ground' (Gen. iv. 3). Again, the tradition which gave Cain a 'chavel-bone' as a lethal weapon (the Wakefield pageant has 'cheek-bone') is of non-biblical origin, and seems to have started life in England, where it is found as early as the ninth century in Old English literature. It was also a popular motif in English manuscript illuminations from the eleventh to the sixteenth century (see Schapiro).

The pageant has a variety of stanza-forms; one of these is a thirteen-line stanza with the same rhyme-scheme as that found in the stanza of the Wakefield pageants (*abababababcdddc*), but with more stressed syllables in each line.

The N. town cycle of forty-two pageants, preserved in a late fifteenth-century manuscript (British Library MS. Cotton Vespasian D. viii), has been edited by Block for the Early English Text Society, and in part by R. T. Davies.

CHARACTERS

GOD

ABEL CAIN ADAM

CAIN AND ABEL

[SCENE I. *Near the dwelling of Adam*]

Abel. I would fain know how I should do
    To serve my Lord God to his pleasing;
    Therefore, Cain, brother, let us now go
    Unto our father without letting,   *delay*
5   Suing him in virtue and in nurture,   *following; breeding*
    To come to the high joy celestial,
    Remembering to be clean and pure,
    For in misrule we might lightly fall   *easily*
    Against heaven king.
10   Let us now do our diligence
    To come to our father's presence;
    Good brother, pass we hence,
    To know for our living.

Cain.   As to my father, let us now tee,   *go*
15   To know what shall be his talking;
    And yet I hold it but vanity
    To go to him for any speaking,
    To lere of his law;
    For if I have good enough plenty,
20   I can be merry, so mote I thee!
    Though my father I never see,
    I give not thereof a haw.

[SCENE II. *The dwelling of Adam*]

Abel. Right sovereign father, seemly sad and sure,
    Ever we thank you in heart, body, and thought,

13 To learn the best way to conduct our lives.
15-18 To find out what he will say; and yet I think it useless to go and
hear him talk, to learn about his rule of life.
20 So may I prosper.
22 i.e. I don't care a jot.
23 Becomingly steadfast and sure.

27

25   And always shall while our life may endure,
      As inwardly in heart it can be sought,
      Both my brother and I.
      Father, I fall unto your knee,
      To know how we shall ruled be
30   For goods that falleth both him and me;
      I would fain wit truly.   *know*

      Adam.   Sons, ye are, to speak naturally,
      The first fruit of kindly engendrure,   *natural procreation*
      Before whom, save your mother and I,
35   Were never none of man's nature;
      And yet were we all of another portraiture,
      As ye have me often heard say soothly.   *truly*
      Wherefore, sons, if ye will live sad and sure,
      First I you counsel most singularly,   *particularly*
40   God for to love and dread;
      And such goods as God hath you sent,
      The first fruit offer to him in sacrifice brent,   *burnt*
      Him ever beseeching with meek intent,   *humble mind*
      In all your works to save and speed.

45 *Abel.*   Gramercy, father, for your good doctrine,   *teaching*
      For as ye us teach so shall we do;
      And, as for me, through God's grace divine
      I will forthwith apply me thereto.
      Cain.   And though me be loath I will now   *I am unwilling*
      also
50   Unto your counsel, father, me incline;
      And yet I say now to you both two,   *the two of you*
      I had liefer go home well for to dine.
      Adam.   Now God grant good sacrifice to you both two;
      He vouchsafe to accept you and all mine,
55   And give you now grace to please him so,

      26 As earnestly as we may.
      29–30 To learn what rule we must follow with regard to the goods that
      have fallen to his share and mine.
      32 To speak of natural generation.
      36 And yet were we (i.e. Adam and Eve) formed in quite a different way.
      44 To preserve and prosper you in all your works.
      52 I had rather go home and eat a good meal.

That ye may come to that bliss that himself is in,
With ghostly grace;
That all your here living   *life here*
May be to his pleasing,
60   And at your hence parting   *death*
To come to good place.

[SCENE III.   *The place of offering*]

Abel.   Almighty God and God full of might,
By whom all thing is made of nought,
To thee my heart is ready dight,
65   For upon thee is all my thought.
O sovereign Lord, reigning in eternity,
With all the meekness that I can or may,
This lamb shall I offer it up to thee:
Accept it, blessed Lord, I thee pray.
70   My gift is but simple, this is no nay,   *undeniably*
But my will is good and ever shall be,
Thee to serve and worship both night and day.
And thereto thy grace grant thou me   *also*
Through thy great mercy,
75   Which, in a lamb's likeness,
Thou shalt for man's wickedness
Once be offered in painfulness,
And die full dolefully.   *with great suffering*

For truly, Lord, thou art most worthy
80   The best to have in each degree;   *every way*
Both best and worst, full certainly,
All is had through grace of thee.
The best sheep, full heartily,   *most willingly*
Amongst my flock that I can see,
85   I tithe it to God of great mercy,   *give it as tithe*
And better would, if better might be.
Even here is my offering:

57 By grace of the Holy Spirit.
64 My heart is made ready for thee.
75-7 Who, in the likeness of a lamb, shall one day for man's wickedness
be sacrificed with pain.

I tithe to thee with right good will
Of the best thou sentest me till;   *to me*
90 Now, gracious God on heaven's hill,
Accept now my tithing.   [*He offers his tithe.*

Cain.   Amongst all fools that go on ground,
I hold that thou be one of the most;
To tithe the best, that is not sound,   *reasonable*
95 And keep the worst that is near lost.   *nearly ruined*
But I more wisely shall work this stound: *act now*
To tithe the worst—and make no boast—
Of all my corns that may be found
In all my fields, both croft and coast;   *hillside*
100 I shall look on every side.
Here I tithe this unthende sheaf: *poor*
Let God take it or else leave;   *leave it*
Though it be to me great reprief,   *shame*
I give no force this tide.

105 *Abel.*   Now Cain, brother, thou dost full ill,
For God thee sent both best and worst;
Therefore thou show to him good will,
And tithe to God ever of the best.
Cain.   In faith, thou showest now a feeble skill;   *reason*
110 It would me hinder and do me grief.   *harm*
What were God the better, thou say me till,
To give him away my best sheaf,
And keep myself the worse?
He will neither eat nor drink,
115 For he doth neither sweat nor swink.   *toil*
Thou showest a feeble reason, methink;
What! thou fonnest as a beast, I guess.   *art foolish*

Abel.   Yet methinketh my wit is good,
To God evermore some love to shew,
120 Of whom we have our daily food,
And else we had but little drew.   *morsel*

97 And keep quiet about it.
100 I shall look everywhere [for the poorest sheaf].
104 I care not now.
111 How would God be the better for it, tell me.

 Cain. Yet methinketh thy wit is wood,   *crazed*
   For of thy lore I find but few.
   I will never the more change my mood
125 For no words that thou dost shew;
   I say I will tithe the worst.
 Abel. Now God that sits in heaven above,
   On whom is set all my whole love,
   This wicked will from thee he shove, *thrust*
130 As it pleaseth him best.

 *Here Abel and Cain burn their tithes, whereupon Cain
 says:*

 Cain. Hark, Abel, brother, what array is *state of affairs*
   this?
   Thy tithing burneth as fire full bright.
   It is to me great wonder, iwis;   *certainly*
   I trow this is now a strange sight.   *think*
135 *Abel.* God's will, forsooth, it is
   That my tithing with fire is light,
   For of the best were my tithes,
   And of the worst thou didst him dight: *prepare*
   Bad thing thou him bede.   *offered*
140 Of the best was my tithing,
   And of the worst was thy offering;
   Therefore God almighty, heaven king,
   Allowed right not thy deed.

 Cain. What, thou stinking losel, and is it so? *scoundrel*
145 Doth God thee love and hateth me?
   Thou shalt be dead, I shall thee slo: *slay*
   Thy Lord, thy God thou shalt never see;
   Tithing more shalt thou never do.
   With this chavel-bone I shall slay thee: *jaw-bone*
150 Thy death is dight, thy days be go. *gone*
   Out of my hands shalt thou not flee;
   With this stroke I thee kill.

  123 For I find but few of your way of thinking.
  143 Did not approve at all of what you did.

Now this boy is slain and dead,   *knave*
Of him I shall never more have dread.
155   He shall hereafter never eat bread;
With this grass I shall him hill.   *conceal*

[*God speaks to Cain*]

God.   Cain, come forth and answer me,
Assoil my question anon right:
Thy brother Abel—where is now he?
160   Have done, and answer me as tite.
Cain.   My brother's keeper who made me?
Since when was I his keeping-knight?   *attendant*
I cannot tell where that he be;
To keep him was I never dight;
165   I know not where he is.
God.   Ah, cursed Cain, thou art untrue,
And for thy deed thou shalt sore rue;   *bitterly repent*
Thy brother's blood, that thou slew,
Asketh vengeance of thy miss.   *misdeed*

170   Thou shalt be cursed on the ground,
Unprofitable whereso thou wend;
Both vain and naughty and nothing sound,
With what thing thou meddle thou shalt it shend.
Cain.   Alas, in woe now am I wound,   *wrapped*
175   Accursed of God as man unkind;   *unnatural*
Of any man if I be found,   *by*
He shall me slay.   I have no friend,
Alas and welaway!
God.   Of what man that thou be slain,   *whatever*
180   He shall have sevenfold more pain;
Him were better to be seen
Alive by night ne day.

158 Answer my question at once.
160 Be quick, and answer me immediately.
164 I was never appointed to take care of him.
171–3 Useless wherever you go; worthless and wicked and unsound,
you shall spoil whatever thing you meddle with.
181–2 He had better not be seen alive by night or day, i.e. he would be
better dead.

Cain.   Alas, alas, whither may I go?
         I dare never see man in the visage;
185   I am wounden as a wretch in woe,
         And cursed of God for my falsage.   *falsehood*
         Unprofitable and vain also,   *useless; worthless*
         In field and town, in street and stage,
         I may never make mirths mo.
190   I wot never whither to take passage;
         I dare not here abide.
         Now will I go wend my way,
         With sore sighing and welaway,   *lamentation*
         To look where that I best may
195   From man's sight me hide.

184 I dare not look any man in the face.
188 *stage,* a raised platform for either the actors or the spectators.
189–90 I can never make merry again.   I don't know where to go.

NOAH'S FLOOD

The Flood is dramatized in all the miracle cycles. Sometimes, as in the Chester and Towneley cycles, there is one pageant for both the Making of the Ark and the Flood; sometimes, as in the York cycle, the two episodes are dealt with in separate pageants. Separation into two pageants presumably took place in the Newcastle cycle, of which the only surviving pageant (the Shipwrights' Play of *Noah's Ark*) is limited to the Making of the Ark. The Trinity House Guild of Master Mariners and Pilots at Hull also acted a Noah play on Plough Monday. The play is now lost, but records of it have survived in the accounts of Trinity House (see Introduction, p. xiii).

Noah's wife in the Chester pageant, as in the Noah pageants of the York and Towneley cycles, is utterly unlike the orthodox theological idea of her as a meek and virtuous prototype of Mary. The comic tradition of the perverse and cantankerous Noah's wife, although it does not appear in medieval drama outside of England, is widespread in European art and folklore (see Mill). Further, it is an old tradition, at least as old as the picture of Noah's Ark in the Junius manuscript (*c.* 1000), which shows the wife standing at the foot of the gangway, and one of her sons trying to persuade her to go on board.

The pageant is mostly written in eight-line stanzas rhyming *aaabcccb* and occasionally *aaabaaab*, with four and three stresses in *a* and *b* respectively. This stanza, known as tail-rhyme, is used throughout the Chester cycle, which has a metrical uniformity not found in the other English cycles. The pageant is especially interesting for its original stage directions; some of these are given in the manuscripts in Latin and some in English. They indicate, among other things, how the animals were represented and how the return of the dove was contrived. It will be seen that the subject of the pageant is appropriate enough to its performers, the water-leaders (water-carriers) and drawers in Dee (drawers of water from the River Dee).

There are two sixteenth-century copies of the Chester Banns and five copies of the cycle itself dating from the late sixteenth and early seventeenth century. One of these, Huntington Library MS. 2 (dated 1591), has been edited by R. M. Lumiansky and D. Mills for the Early English Text Society.

NOAH'S FLOOD

*And first in some high place, or in the clouds if it may
be, God speaketh unto Noah standing without the
Ark with all his family.*

God.　I, God, that all the world have wrought,
　　Heaven and earth, and all of nought,　　　　*from nothing*
　　I see my people, in deed and thought,
　　Are set foully in sin.
5　My ghost shall not leng in man,
　　That through fleshly liking is my fone,
　　But till six score years be gone,
　　To look if they will blin.

　　Man that I made I will destroy,
10　Beast, worm, and fowl to fly;
　　For on earth they do me noy,　　　　　　　*harm*
　　The folk that are thereon.
　　It harms me so heartfully,
　　The malice now that can multiply,
15　That sore it grieveth me inwardly
　　That ever I made man.

　　Therefore, Noah, my servant free,　　　　　*noble*
　　That righteous man art, as I see,
　　A ship soon thou shalt make thee
20　Of trees dry and light.
　　Little chambers therein thou make;
　　And binding-slitch also thou take:
　　Within and out thou ne slake
　　To anoint it through all thy might.

5–8　My spirit shall remain in mankind, who are my foes because of their
sensuality, only till six score years are gone, to see if they will stop [sinning].
10　Reptile, and bird flying.
13–14　The malice that now doth multiply wounds me so deeply in my
heart.
22　*binding-slitch*, pitch used for stopping up the seams of a ship.
23–4　Do not slacken your efforts to anoint it inside and out with all
your might.

37

25   **Three** hundred cubits it shall be long,
    And fifty of breadth, to make it strong;
    Of height fifty.   The met thou fong;
    Thus measure it about.   *all round*
    One window work through thy wit,
30   One cubit of length and breadth make it;
    Upon the side a door shall sit,   *be placed*
    For to come in and out.

    Eating-places thou make also,
    Three roofed chambers on a row;
35   For with water I think to flow   *drown*
    Man that I can make.   *did make*
    Destroyed all the world shall be,
    Save thou; thy wife, thy sons three,
    And all their wives also with thee
40   Shall saved be for thy sake.

    Noah.   Ah, Lord, I thank thee loud and still,   *at all times*
    That to me art in such will,
    And sparest me and my house to spill,
    As now I soothly find.
45   Thy bidding, Lord, I shall fulfil,
    And never more thee grieve ne grill,   *nor offend*
    That such grace has sent me till   *to me*
    Among all mankind.   *above*
                         [To his family :

    Have done, you men and women all!
50   Help, for aught that may befall,
    To work this ship, chamber and hall,   *build*
    As God hath bidden us do.
    Shem.   Father, I am all ready boun: *prepared*
    An axe I have, by my crown,
55   As sharp as any in all this town,
    For to go thereto.   *to it*

    27 Take the measurement yourself.
    29 Make a window by your skill.
    34 One on top of another.
    42–3 That art so minded towards me, and refrainest from destroying me
and my household.
    50 Whatever happens.
    54 *by my crown*, an asseveration.

Ham. I have a hatchet wondrous keen
  To bite well, as may be seen;   *cut*
  A better grounden, as I ween, *sharpened; think*
60 Is not in all this town.
 Japheth. And I can well make a pin, *peg*
  And with this hammer knock it in;
  Go and work without more din,
  And I am ready boun.

65 *N's Wife.* And we shall bring timber to, *to this place*
  For we mun nothing else do;   *may*
  Women be weak to underfo   *undertake*
  Any great travail.   *labour*
 S's Wife. Here is a good hackstock; *chopping-block*
70 On this you may hew and knock;
  Shall none be idle in this flock,
  Ne now may no man fail.

H's Wife. And I will go to gather slitch,
  The ship for to caulk and pitch;
75 Anointed it must be every stitch, *part*
  Board, tree, and pin.   *beam*
 J's Wife. And I will gather chips here
  To make a fire for you in fere, *you all*
  And for to dight your dinner, *prepare*
80 Against you come in.

*Then they make signs as if they were working with
  different tools.*

Noah. Now, in the name of God, I will begin
  To make the ship that we shall in, *live in*
  That we be ready for to swim *float*
  At the coming of the flood.
85 These boards I join here together,
  To keep us safe from the weather,
  That we may row both hither and thither,
  And safe be from this flood.

72 Nor may any one now fail [to do his part].

        Of this tree will I make the mast,
90   Tied with cables that will last,
        With a sail-yard for each blast,
        And each thing in their kind;
        With topcastle and bowsprit,
        With cords and ropes, I have all **meet**   *fit*
95   To sail forth at the next wet;   *downpour*
        This ship is at an end.   *finished*

        Then Noah with all his family again make signs of
            working with different tools.

        Wife, in this castle we shall be kept;   *kept safe*
        My children and thou, I would, in leapt.
    N's Wife.   In faith, Noah, I had as lief thou slept.
100   For all thy frankish fare,
        I will not do after thy rede.
    Noah.   Good wife, do now as I thee bid.
    N's Wife.   By Christ, not ere I see more need,
        Though thou stand all the day and stare.

105 *Noah.*   Lord, that women be crabbed ay,   *always perverse*
        And never are meek, that dare I say.
        This is well seen by me to-day,
        In witness of you each one.
        Good wife, let be all this bere   *clamour*
110   That thou makes in this place here;
        For all they ween thou art master—
        And so thou art, by St John!

        91 *sail-yard*, a yard-arm on which the sail is spread.
        92 And every kind of thing [needed].
        93 *topcastle*, a fortified platform at the mast-head.
        97 *castle*, a raised structure on the deck of a ship.
        98 I would like my children and you to hurry in.
        99–101 I would as soon you slept. For all your polite behaviour,
    won't do as you advise.
        108 As each of you (i.e. the audience) has witnessed.
        111 *they*, i.e. the audience.

[*God speaks to Noah*]

	God. Noah, take thou thy meny,	*household*
	And in the ship hie that thou be;	
115	For none so righteous man to me	
	Is now on earth living.	
	Of clean beasts with thee thou take	
	Seven and seven, ere thou slake;	*by sevens; stop*
	He and she, make to make,	*mate*
120	Belive in that thou bring.	

	Of beasts unclean two and two,	*by twos*
	Male and female, without mo;	*and no more*
	Of clean fowls seven also,	*birds*
	The he and she together;	
125	Of fowls unclean two and no more,	
	As I of beasts said before,	
	That shall be saved through my lore,	*instruction*
	Against I send the weather.	*tempest*

	Of all meats that must be eaten	*food*
130	Into the ship look there be gotten,	
	For that no way may be forgotten;	
	And do all this bedene,	*at once*
	To sustain man and beast therein	
	Ay till the water cease and blin.	
135	This world is filled full of sin,	
	And that is now well seen.	*easy to see*

	Seven days be yet coming:	
	You shall have space them in to bring;	*time*
	After that it is my liking	*pleasure*
140	Mankind for to noy.	*harm*
	Forty days and forty nights	
	Rain shall fall for their unrights;	*iniquities*
	And that I have made through my mights	
	Now think I to destroy.	

114–15 And hasten on board ship; for no man so righteous in my sight.
120 [See] that you quickly bring in.
131 For they must on no account be forgotten.
134 All the time till the flood-waters cease and come to an end.
143 And that which I made through my might.

145 *Noah.*   Lord, at your bidding I am bain;   *ready*
           Since no other grace will gain,
           It will I fulfil fain,   *gladly*
           For gracious I thee find.
           A hundred winters and twenty
150   This ship-making tarried have I,
           If through amendment any mercy
           Would fall unto mankind.

                                        [*To his family:*

           Have done, you men and women all!
           Hie you lest this water fall,
155   That each beast were in his stall,
           And into the ship brought.
           Of clean beasts seven shall be,
           Of unclean two; this God bade me.
           This flood is nigh, well may we see;
160   Therefore tarry you nought.

           *Then Noah shall go into the Ark with all his family,
           his wife except, and the Ark must be boarded round
           about, and on the boards all the beasts and fowls
           hereafter rehearsed must be painted, that these words
           may agree with the pictures.*

           Shem.   Sir, here are lions, leopards in,   *inside*
           Horses, mares, oxen, and swine;
           Goats, calves, sheep, and kine
           Here sitten thou may see.   *lying down*
165 *Ham.*   Camels, asses men may find,
           Buck, doe, hart, and hind;
           And beasts of all manner kind
           Here be, as thinketh me.   *it seems to me*

           146. Since nothing else will win grace.
           149–52 I have prolonged this shipbuilding for 120 years, [to see] if
           mankind would mend its ways and be granted mercy.
           154–5 Hurry, lest the water pour down, so that each beast may be in
           its stall.
           167 Of every sort and kind.

Japh.   Take here cats and dogs too,
170 Otter, fox, fulmart also;   *polecat*
Hares hopping gaily can go
Have cole here for to eat.   *cabbage*
N's Wife.   And here are bears, wolves set,   *lying*
Apes, owls, marmoset,
175 Weasels, squirrels, and ferret;
Here they eat their meat.

S's Wife.   Yet more beasts are in this house:
Here cats maken it full crouse;
Here a ratton, here a mouse,   *rat*
180 They stand nigh together.
H's Wife.   And here are fowls, less and more: *small and big*
Herons, cranes, and bittor,   *bittern*
Swans, peacocks; and them before
Meat for this weather.

185 *J's Wife.*   Here are cocks, kites, crows,
Rooks, ravens, many rows,   *row upon row*
Ducks, curlews, whoever knows
Each one in his kind;
And here are doves, digs, drakes,   *ducks*
190 Redshanks running through the lakes;
And each fowl that leden makes   *song*
In this ship men may find.

Noah.   Wife, come in!   Why stands thou there?
Thou art ever froward, that dare I swear.   *perverse*
195 Come in, on God's half!   Time it were,
For fear lest that we drown.
N's Wife.   Yea, sir, set up your sail,
And row forth with evil hail,
For, without any fail,   *doubt*
200 I will not out of this town.

171 Hares which go hopping gaily.
178 Are having a lively time.
183-4 And in front of them is food for [them to eat during] the tempest.
187-8 For anyone who knows each species.
195 Come in, for God's sake!   It 's high time.
198 With ill success, i.e. and bad luck to you.
200 I will not leave this town.

But I have my gossips every one,   *unless; friends*
One foot further I will not gone;   *go*
They shall not drown, by St John,
And I may save their life.   *if*
205 They loved me full well, by Christ;
But thou wilt let them in thy chest,
Else row forth, Noah, whither thou list,
And get thee a new wife.

Noah. Shem, son, lo! thy mother is wrow: *angry*
210 Forsooth, such another I do not know.
Shem. Father, I shall fetch her in, I trow,   *think*
Without any fail.   [*He goes to his mother.*
Mother, my father after thee sent,
And bids thee into yonder ship wend.   *go*
215 Look up and see the wind,
For we be ready to sail.

N's Wife. Son, go again to him, and say
I will not come therein to-day.
Noah. Come in, wife, in twenty devils way,
220 Or else stand there without.
Ham. Shall we all fetch her in?
Noah. Yea, sons, in Christ's blessing and mine;   *with*
I would you hied you betime,
For of this flood I am in doubt.   *afraid*

225 *Gossip.* [*To Wife*] The flood comes fleeting in full   *flowing*
fast,
On every side it spreads full far;
For fear of drowning I am aghast;
Good gossip, let us draw near.

And let us drink ere we depart,
230 For oft-times we have done so;
For at a draught thou drink'st a quart,
And so will I do ere I go.

206–7 Unless you will let them into your chest (i.e. the Ark), row away, Noah, where you like.
219 In the devil's name.
223 I would like you to hurry and waste no time.

N's Wife.   Here is a pottle of Malmsey, good and
    strong;
    It will rejoice both heart and tongue;
235   Though Noah thinks us never so long,
    Yet we will drink alike.

    Japh.   Mother, we pray you altogether—
    For we are here your own childer—
    Come into the ship for fear of the weather,
240   For his love that you bought!
    N's Wife.   That will I not, for all your call,   *bidding*
    But I have my gossips all.
    Shem.   In faith, mother, yet you shall,
    Whether you will or nought.

                      Then she shall go.

245 *Noah.*   Welcome, wife, into this boat.
    N's Wife.   And have thou that for thy note!

                  She boxes him on the ear.

    Noah.   Aha! marry, this is hot!
    It is good to be still.   *peaceful*
    Ah, children, methinks my boat removes;   *moves*
250   Our tarrying here hugely me grieves.
    Over the land the water spreads;
    God do as he will!

    Ah, great God that art so good,
    That works not thy will is wood.
255   Now all this world is on a flood,
    As I well see in sight.
    This window will I shut anon,
    And into my chamber will I gone,
    Till this water, so great one,
260   Be slaked through thy might.   *lessened*

233 *pottle*, a pot containing two quarts; *Malmsey*, a strong sweet wine.
236 i.e. a quart each.
240 For love of Him who redeemed you.
246 Have that for your trouble.
247 I'm catching it hot.
254 He who does not thy will is mad.
256 As I plainly see with my own eyes.
259 Till this flood, which is so great.

Then Noah shall shut the window of the Ark, and for a
little space within board he shall be silent, and after-
wards opening the window and looking round about,
saying :

Now forty days are fully gone,
Send a raven I will anon,
If aught-where earth, tree, or stone
Be dry in any place;
265 And if this fowl come not again,
It is a sign, sooth to sain,   *to speak truly*
That dry it is on hill or plain,
And God hath done some grace.   *granted*

Then he shall send forth a raven; and taking a dove in
his hand let him say :

Ah, Lord, wherever this raven be,
270 Somewhere is dry, well I see;
But yet a dove, by my lewty,   *faith*
After I will send.
Thou wilt turn again to me,
For of all fowls that may flee,   *fly*
275 Thou art most meek and hend.   *gentle*

Then he shall send forth a dove; and there shall be in
the ship another dove bearing an olive-branch in her
mouth, which Noah shall let down from the mast by a
cord in his hand; and afterwards let Noah say :

Ah, Lord, blessed be thou ay,
That me hast comfort thus to-day;   *comforted*
By this sight I may well say
This flood begins to cease.
280 My sweet dove to me brought has
A branch of olive from some place;
This betokeneth God has done us some grace,
And is a sign of peace.

263 [To see] if anywhere.

Ah, Lord, honoured must thou be!
285   All earth drys now, I see;
But yet, till thou command me,
Hence will I not hie.   *hasten*
All this water is away;
Therefore, as soon as I may,
290   Sacrifice I shall do, in fay,   *faith*
To thee devoutly.

[*God speaks to Noah*]

God.   Noah, take thy wife anon,
And thy children every one;
Out of the ship thou shalt gone,
295   And they all with thee.
Beasts and all that can fly
Out anon they shall hie,
On earth to grow and multiply;
I will that it so be.

300 *Noah.*   Lord, I thank thee through thy might;   *for*
Thy bidding shall be done in hight,   *haste*
And as fast as I may dight   *make ready*
I will do thee honour,
And to thee offer sacrifice;
305   Therefore come, in all wise,
For of these beasts that be his,
Offer I will this store.   *great number*

*Then going out of the Ark with all his family he shall
take his animals and birds and offer them in sacrifice.*

Lord God in majesty,
That such grace hast granted me,
310   Where all was lorn, safe to be,   *lost*
Therefore now am I boun,   *ready*
My wife, my children, and my meny,   *household*
With sacrifice to honour thee;
Of beasts, fowls, as thou mayst see,
315   I offer here right soon.

305 By all means. (Noah is addressing his family.)

[*God speaks to Noah*]

    God.   Noah, to me thou art full able,   *most compliant*
        And thy sacrifice acceptable;
        For I have found thee true and stable,   *because*
        On thee now must I min:
320   Wary earth will I no more
        For man's sin that grieves me sore;
        For of youth man full yore
        Has been inclined to sin.

        You shall now grow and multiply,
325   And earth again you edify;   *shall build up*
        Each beast, and fowl that may fly
        Shall be afraid of you;
        And fish in sea that may fleet   *float*
        Shall sustain you, I you beheet;   *promise*
330   To eat of them you ne let
        That clean be you may know.

        Thereas you have eaten before   *whereas*
        Grass and roots, since you were bore,   *born*
        Of clean beasts now, less and more,
335   I give you leave to eat,
        Save blood and flesh, both in fere,   *together*
        Of wrong-dead carrion that is here;
        Eat not of that in no manner,
        For that ay you shall let.

340   Manslaughter also you shall flee,   *shun*
        For that is not pleasant to me;   *pleasing*
        That shedeth blood, he or she,
        Aught-where amongst mankin,   *mankind*

    319–23 I must now be mindful of you: I will no more curse the earth
because of man's sin that grieves me sorely; for from his youth man has
long been inclined to sin.
    330–1 Do not forbear to eat those that you know to be clean.
    337 Wrongly dead, i.e. killed in an improper manner.
    338–9 Do not eat that at all, for you must always leave that alone.
    342 Whoever sheds blood.

That blood foully shed shall be
345 And vengeance have, that men shall see;
Therefore beware now all ye,
You fall not in that sin.

A forward, Noah, with thee I make,   *covenant*
And all thy seed for thy sake,
350 Of such vengeance for to slake,
For now I have my will.
Here I beheet thee a hest
That man, woman, fowl ne beast,
With water, while the world shall last,
355 I will no more spill.   *destroy*

My bow between you and me   *rainbow*
In the firmament shall be,
By very token that you may see
That such vengeance shall cease,
360 That man ne woman never more
Be wasted by water, as is before;
But for sin that grieveth me sore,
Therefore this vengeance was.

Where clouds in the welkin been,
365 That ilk bow shall be seen,   *same*
In token that my wrath and teen   *anger*
Shall never thus wroken be.   *wreaked*
The string is turned toward you,
And toward me is bent the bow,
370 That such weather shall never show;
And this beheet I thee.

My blessing now I give thee here,
To thee, Noah, my servant dear,
For vengeance shall no more appear;
375 And now farewell, my darling dear.

350 To lessen such vengeance, i.e. such vengeance as I have just taken.
352 Here I promise you.
358 As a true sign.
361 Shall be destroyed by water, as happened before.
364 Are in the sky.
370 [As a sign] that such bad weather shall never be seen.

ABRAHAM AND ISAAC

Although there is no way of proving that this play once formed part of a cycle, it looks like an ordinary craft pageant and indeed is similar to part of the *Sacrifice of Isaac* in the Chester cycle. To account for the similarities in structure and language between the two plays it must be supposed that one is derived from the other, or both from a common original. But the Brome play is the better of the two, despite its irregular rhymes and metres, and it seems likely that the central part of the Chester pageant is a corrupt version of the central part of the original Brome play (see Severs).

Most critics are agreed that the Brome play is superior to the pageants on the same theme in the four English cycles and to the Abraham and Isaac play contained in a fifteenth-century manuscript at Trinity College, Dublin. E. K. Chambers (*English Literature at the Close of the Middle Ages*, pp. 43–4) is alone in dismissing it as 'dull, and mainly in doggerel.'

The Brome play, which is preserved in a late fifteenth-century manuscript from Brome Hall in Suffolk, is now in Yale University Library. It has been edited by N. Davis for the Early English Text Society.

CHARACTERS

GOD

ABRAHAM   ANGEL

ISAAC   DOCTOR

ABRAHAM AND ISAAC

Abraham.   Father of heaven omnipotent,
    With all my heart to thee I call:
    Thou hast given me both land and rent,   *revenue*
    And my livelihood thou hast me sent;
5   I thank thee highly, evermore, of all.   *for*

    First of the earth thou madest Adam,
    And Eve also to be his wife;
    All other creatures of them two came.
    And now thou hast granted to me, Abraham,
10 Here in this land to lead my life.

    In my age thou hast granted me this,
    That this young child with me shall won;   *dwell*
    I love nothing so much, iwis,   *indeed*
    Except thine own self, dear Father of bliss,
15 As Isaac here, my own sweet son.

    I have divers children mo,   *more*
    The which I love not half so well;
    This fair sweet child he cheers me so
    In every place where that I go,
20 That no disease here may I feel.   *discomfort*

    And therefore, Father of heaven, I thee pray
    For his health and also for his grace;
    Now, Lord, keep him both night and day,
    That never disease nor no affray   *fear*
25 Come to my child in no place.

Now come on, Isaac, my own sweet child;
Go we home and take our rest.
Isaac.   Abraham, my own father so mild,
To follow you I am full prest,   *ready*
30   Both early and late.
Abr.   Come on, sweet child.   I love thee best
Of all the children that ever I begat.

[SCENE II.   *Heaven*]

God.   My angel, fast hie thee thy way,   *hasten*
And unto middle-earth anon thou go;   *the earth*
35   Abraham's heart now will I essay,
Whether that he be steadfast or no.

Say I commanded him for to take
Isaac, his young son, that he loves so well,
And with his blood sacrifice he make,
40   If any of my friendship he will feel.

Show him the way unto the hill
Where that his sacrifice shall be;
I shall essay now his good will,
Whether he loves better his child or me.
45   All men shall take example by him
My commandments how they shall keep.

[SCENE III.   *Abraham's dwelling*]

Abr.   Now, Father of heaven, that formed all thing,
My prayers I make to thee again,
For this day my tender-offering   *burnt-offering*
50   Here must I give to thee, certain.   *assuredly*
Ah, Lord God, almighty King,
What manner beast will make thee most fain?   *glad*
If I had thereof very knowing,   *true knowledge*
It should be done with all my main   *strength*
55   Full soon anon;
To do thy pleasing on a hill,   *pleasure*
Verily it is my will,
Dear Father, God in Trinity.

[Enter Angel]

Angel.   Abraham, Abraham, wilt thou rest?
60   Our Lord commandeth thee for to take
       Isaac, thy young son, that thou lovest best,
       And with his blood sacrifice that thou make.
       Into the land of vision thou go,
       And offer thy child unto thy Lord;
65   I shall thee lead and show also.
       Unto God's hest, Abraham, accord,   *command*
       And follow me upon this green.
Abr.   Welcome to me be my Lord's sand,   *messenger*
       And his hest I will not withstand;
70   Yet Isaac, my young son in land,   *on earth*
       A full dear child to me has been.

       I had liefer, if God had been pleased,   *rather*
       For to have forborne all the goods that I have,   *lost*
       Than Isaac my son should have been diseased,   *molested*
75   So God in heaven my soul mote save!   *may*

       I loved never thing so much in earth,
       And now I must the child go kill.
       Ah, Lord God, my conscience is strongly stirred!
       And yet, my dear Lord, I am sore afeard
80   To grudge anything against your will.

       I love my child as my life,
       But yet I love my God much more;
       For though my heart would wake any strife,
       Yet will I not spare for child nor wife,
85   But do after my Lord's lore.   *instruction*

       Though I love my son never so well,
       Yet smite off his head soon I shall.
       Ah, Father of heaven, to thee I kneel;
       A hard death my son shall feel,
90   For to honour thee, Lord, withal.

63 i.e. the land of Moriah (Genesis xxii. 2).
80 To complain at all against your will.
83 Should rebel.

Ang.   Abraham, Abraham, this is well said!
And all these commandments look that thou keep,
But in thy heart be nothing dismayed.   [*Exit.*
Abr.   Nay, nay, forsooth, I hold me well paid
95   To please my God with the best that I have.

For though my heart be heavily set   *hard*
To see the blood of my own dear son,
Yet for all this I will not let,   *desist*
But Isaac, my son, I will go fet,   *fetch*
100   And come as fast as ever we can.

Now, Isaac, my own son dear,
Where art thou, child?   Speak to me.
Isaac.   My father, sweet father, I am here,
And make my prayers to the Trinity.

105 *Abr.*   Rise up, my child, and fast come hither,
My gentle bairn that art so wise,
For we two, child, must go together,
And unto my Lord make sacrifice.

Isaac.   I am full ready, my father, lo!
110   Even at your hands I stand right here,
And whatsoever ye bid me do,
It shall be done with glad cheer,
Full well and fine. /   *fully*
Abr.   Ah, Isaac, my own son so dear,
115   God's blessing I give thee, and mine.

Hold this faggot upon thy back,
And here myself fire shall bring.
Isaac.   Father, all this here will I pack;
I am full fain to do your bidding.
120 *Abr.* [*Aside*]   Ah, Lord of heaven, my hands I wring!
This child's words all to-wound my heart.   *deeply wound*

94 I think myself well satisfied.

Now, Isaac, son, go we our way
Unto yon mount, with all our main.
 Isaac. Go we, my dear father. As fast as I may,
125 To follow you I am full fain,
 Although I be slender.   *weak*
 Abr. [*Aside*] Ah, Lord, my heart breaketh on twain!
 This child's words, they be so tender.

     [SCENE IV. *The hill*]

 Abr. Ah, Isaac, son, anon lay it down;
130 No longer upon thy back it hold,
 For I must make ready boun   *prepared*
 To honour my Lord God as I should.

 Isaac. Lo, my dear father, where it is.
 To cheer you always I draw me near;
135 But, father, I marvel sore of this,   *at*
 Why that ye make this heavy cheer.

 And also, father, evermore dread I:
 Where is your quick beast that ye should kill? *live*
 Both fire and wood we have ready,
140 But quick beast have we none on this hill.

 A quick beast, I wot well, must be dead *know*
 Your sacrifice for to make.
 Abr. Dread thee not, my child, I thee rede; *advise*
 Our Lord will send me unto this stead *place*
145 Some manner a beast for to take,   *kind of*
 Through his sweet sand.   *messenger*
 Isaac. Yea, father, but my heart beginneth to quake
 To see that sharp sword in your hand.

 Why bear ye your sword drawn so?
150 Of your countenance I have much wonder.
 Abr. [*Aside*] Ah, Father of heaven, so I am woe!
 This child here breaks my heart asunder.

  129 *it*, i.e. the faggot.
  136 Why you look so sad.
  151 So sad am I!

Isaac.   Tell me, my dear father, ere that ye cease,
 Bear ye your sword drawn for me?
155 *Abr.*   Ah, Isaac, sweet son, peace! peace!
 For, iwis, thou break'st my heart on three.

Isaac.   Now truly, somewhat, father, ye think,
 That ye mourn thus more and more.
Abr. [*Aside*]   Ah, Lord of heaven, thy grace let
  sink,   *descend*
160 For my heart was never half so sore.

Isaac.   I pray you, father, ye let me that wit, *know*
 Whether shall I have any harm or no.
Abr.   Iwis, sweet son, I may not tell thee yet;
 My heart is now so full of woe.

165 *Isaac.*   Dear father, I pray you, hide it not from me,
 But some of your thought that ye tell me.
Abr.   Ah, Isaac, Isaac, I must kill thee!
Isaac.   Kill me, father?   Alas, what have I done?

If I have trespassed against you aught, *at all*
170 With a yard ye may make me full mild; *rod*
 And with your sharp sword kill me nought,
 For iwis, father, I am but a child.

Abr.   I am full sorry thy blood for to spill,
 But truly, my child, I may not choose.
175 *Isaac.*   Now I would my mother were here on this hill!
 She would kneel for me on both her knees
 To save my life.
 And since that my mother is not here,
 I pray you, father, change your cheer,
180 And kill me not with your knife.

Abr.   Forsooth, son, but if I thee kill, *unless*
 I should grieve God right sore, I dread.
 It is his commandment and also his will
 That I should do this same deed.

157 You have something on your mind.
179 Change your expression, i.e. don't look so sad.

185   He commanded me, son, for certain,
       To make my sacrifice with thy blood.
    Isaac.   And is it God's will that I should be slain?
    Abr.   Yea, truly, Isaac, my son so good;
       And therefore my hands I wring.

190 *Isaac.*   Now, father, against my Lord's will
       I will never grudge, loud nor still;
       He might have sent me a better destiny
       If it had been his pleasure.

    Abr.   Forsooth, son, but if I did this deed,
195   Grievously displeased our Lord will be.
    Isaac.   Nay, nay, father, God forbid
       That ever ye should grieve him for me.   *offend*

       Ye have other children, one or two,
       The which ye should love well by kind.   *nature*
200   I pray you, father, make ye no woe;
       For, be I once dead and from you go,
       I shall be soon out of your mind.

       Therefore do our Lord's bidding,
       And when I am dead, then pray for me.
205   But, good father, tell ye my mother nothing;
       Say that I am in another country dwelling.
    Abr.   Ah, Isaac, Isaac, blessed mote thou be!

       My heart beginneth strongly to rise,   *rebel*
       To see the blood of thy blessed body.
210 *Isaac.*   Father, since it may be no other wise,
       Let it pass over as well as I.

       But, father, ere I go unto my death,
       I pray you bless me with your hand.   [*Kneels.*
    Abr.   Now, Isaac, with all my breath

    191 I will never complain at all.
    209 [At the thought of] seeing.
    210-11 Since it may not be otherwise, get it over without complaining,
just as I intend to do.

215 My blessing I give thee upon this land,   *earth*
And God's also thereto, iwis.
Isaac, Isaac, son, up thou stand,
Thy fair sweet mouth that I may kiss.

Isaac.   Now farewell, my own father so fine,
220 And greet well my mother in earth;
But I pray you, father, to hide my eyne,   *eyes*
That I see not the stroke of your sharp sword,
That my flesh shall defile.
Abr.   Son, thy words make me to weep full sore;
225 Now, my dear son Isaac, speak no more.
Isaac.   Ah, my own dear father, wherefore?
We shall speak together here but a while.   *short time*

And since that I must needs be dead,
Yet, my dear father, to you I pray,
230 Smite but few strokes at my head,
And make an end as soon as ye may,
And tarry not too long.
Abr.   Thy meek words, child, make me affray;   *frighten me*
So 'Welaway!' may be my song,

235 Except all only God's will.
Ah, Isaac, my own sweet child,
Yet kiss me again upon this hill!
In all this world is none so mild.

Isaac.   Now truly, father, all this tarrying
240 It doth my heart but harm;   *nothing but*
I pray you, father, make an ending.
Abr.   Come up, sweet son, unto my arm.

I must bind thy hands two,
Although thou be never so mild.
245 *Isaac.*   Ah, mercy, father! why should ye do so?
Abr.   That thou shouldst not let, my child.   *hinder*

234–5 'Alas!' may be my song (i.e. I may well have cause to mourn),
except by God's will alone.

Isaac. Nay, iwis, father, I will not let you.
Do on for me your will;
And on the purpose that ye have set you,
250 For God's love keep it forth still.

I am full sorry this day to die,
But yet I keep not my God to grieve;   *wish*
Do on your list for me hardily,
My fair sweet father, I give you leave.

255 But, father, I pray you evermore,
Tell ye my mother no deal.   *not at all*
If she wost it, she would weep full sore,   *knew*
For iwis, father, she loveth me full well;
God's blessing mote she have!

260 Now farewell, my mother so sweet!
We two be like no more to meet.
Abr. Ah, Isaac, son, thou mak'st me to greet,   *weep*
And with thy words thou distemper'st me.   *upset*

Isaac. Iwis, father, I am sorry to grieve you.
265 I cry you mercy of that I have done,
And of all trespass that ever I did move you;
Now, dear father, forgive me that I have done.
God of heaven be with me!

Abr. Ah, dear child, leave off thy moans!
270 In all thy life thou grieved me never once;
Now blessed be thou, body and bones,
That ever thou were bred and born!
Thou hast been to me child full good.
But iwis, child, though I mourn never so fast,   *deeply*
275 Yet must I needs here at the last
In this place shed all thy blood.

248-50 Go on and do with me what you will; and for the love of God
keep to the purpose you have set yourself.
253 Boldly do as you like with me.
266 And for all the sins of mine that ever angered you.
271 i.e. wholly.

Therefore, my dear son, here shall thou lie;
                    [*Lifts him on to the altar.*

Unto my work I must me stead.   *apply myself*
Iwis I had as lief myself to die,
280   If God will be pleased with my deed,
And my own body for to offer.
Isaac.   Ah, mercy, father, mourn ye no more!
Your weeping maketh my heart sore,
As my own death that I shall suffer.

285   Your kerch, fader, about my eyes ye wind.   *kerchief*
Abr.   So I shall, my sweetest child in earth.
Isaac.   Now yet, good father, have this in mind,
And smite me not often with your sharp sword,
But hastily that it be sped.   *done quickly*

Here Abraham laid a cloth on Isaac's face, thus saying:

290 *Abr.*   Now farewell, my child, so full of grace.
Isaac.   Ah, father, father, turn downward my face,
For of your sharp sword I am ever adread.   *afraid*

Abr.   To do this deed I am full sorry,
But, Lord, thy hest I will not withstand.
295 *Isaac.*   Ah, Father of heaven, to thee I cry:
Lord, receive me into thy hand!

Abr.   Lo, now is the time come, certain,
That my sword in his neck shall bite.
Ah, Lord, my heart riseth thereagain;   *against it*
300   I may not find it in my heart to smite;
My heart will not now thereto.
Yet fain I would work my Lord's will;
But this young innocent lieth so still,
I may not find it in my heart him to kill.
305   Oh, Father of heaven, what shall I do?

279–81 Indeed I would as willingly die myself, and offer my own body,
if God would be pleased with my action.
301 My heart now will not allow me to do it.

Isaac.   Ah, mercy, father, why tarry ye so,
          And let me lie thus long on this heath?
          Now would I to God the stroke were do!   *done*
          Father, I pray you heartily, short me of my woe,
310   And let me not look after my death.

Abr.   Now, heart, why wouldest not thou break in
             three?
         Yet shall thou not make me to my God unmild.   *ungracious*
         I will no longer let for thee,
         For that my God aggrieved would be;
315   Now hold the stroke, my own dear child.   *receive*

         *Here Abraham made as if to strike, and the Angel took
             the sword in his hand suddenly.*

Ang.   I am an angel, thou mayst see blithe,   *gladly*
         That from heaven to thee is sent.
         Our Lord thank thee a hundred sithe   *times*
         For the keeping of his commandment.

320   He knoweth thy will and also thy heart,
         That thou dreadest him above all thing;
         And some of thy heaviness for to depart,
         A fair ram yonder I gan bring.   *did*

         He standeth tied, lo, among the briars.
325   Now, Abraham, amend thy mood,
         For Isaac, thy young son that here is,
         This day thou shall not shed his blood.

         Go, make thy sacrifice with yon ram.
         Now farewell, blessed Abraham,
330   For unto heaven I go now home;
         The way is full gain.   *straight*
         Take up thy son so free.   [*Exit.*   *noble*

309–10 I pray you with all my heart to shorten my sorrow, and not
leave me to look forward fearfully to my death.
313 Delay for your sake.
322 And to banish some of your sorrow.
325 Be cheerful.

Abr.   Ah, Lord, I thank thee of thy great grace!   *for*
    Now am I eathed in divers wise.
335   Arise up, Isaac, my dear son, arise;
    Arise up, sweet child, and come to me.

Isaac.   Ah, mercy, father!   Why smite ye nought?
    Ah, smite on, father, once with your knife.
   Abr.   Peace, my sweet sir, and take no thought,
340   For our Lord of heaven hath granted thy life
    By his angel now,

    That thou shalt not die this day, son, truly.
   Isaac.   Ah, father, full glad then were I—
    Iwis, fader, I say, iwis!—
345   If this tale were true.
   Abr.   A hundred times, my son fair of hue,
    For joy thy mouth now will I kiss.

Isaac.   Ah, my dear father, Abraham,
    Will not God be wroth that we do thus?
350 *Abr.*   No, no, hardily, my sweet son,   *certainly*
    For yon same ram he hath us sent
    Hither down to us.

    Yon beast shall die in thy stead,
    In the worship of our Lord alone.
355   Go, fetch him hither, my child, indeed.
   Isaac.   Father, I will go hent him by the head,   *seize*
    And bring yon beast with me anon.

    Ah, sheep, sheep, blessed mote thou be,
    That ever thou were sent down hither!
360   Thou shalt this day die for me
    In the worship of the holy Trinity.
    Now come fast and go we together
    To my father in hie;   *haste*
    Though thou be never so gentle and good,
365   Yet had I liefer thou shed'st thy blood,
    Iwis, sheep, than I.

334 Now am I greatly comforted.

Lo, father, I have brought here full smart   *promptly*
This gentle sheep, and him to you I give;
But, Lord God, I thank thee with all my heart,
370 For I am glad that I shall live,
And kiss once my dear mother.
   Abr. Now be right merry, my sweet child,
For this quick beast that is so mild
Here I shall present before all other.   *offer*

375 *Isaac.* And I will fast begin to blow;
This fire shall burn a full good speed.
But, father, will I stoop down low,   *if I will*
Ye will not kill me with your sword, I trow?
   Abr. No, hardily, sweet son. Have no dread;
380 My mourning is past.
   Isaac. Yea, but I would that sword were in a gleed,   *fire*
For iwis, father, it makes me full ill   *badly frightened*
   aghast.

*Here Abraham made his offering, kneeling and saying
   thus :*

   Abr. Now, Lord God of heaven in Trinity,
Almighty God omnipotent,
385 My offering I make in the worship of thee,
And with this quick beast I thee present.
Lord, receive thou my intent,
As thou art God and ground of our grace.

[*God speaks to Abraham*]

   God. Abraham, Abraham, well mote thou speed,
390 And Isaac, thy young son thee by!
Truly, Abraham, for this deed
I shall multiply your bothers seed   *both your*
As thick as stars be in the sky,
Both more and less;
395 And as thick as gravel in the sea,
So thick multiplied your seed shall be;
This grant I you for your goodness.

394 Both big and small, i.e. all.

Of you shall come fruit great wone,   *quantity*
And ever be in bliss without end.
400 For ye dread me as God alone,   *because*
And keep my commandments every one,
My blessing I give, wheresoever ye wend.

Abr. Lo, Isaac, my son, how think ye
By this work that we have wrought?   *of*
405 Full glad and blithe we may be,
Against the will of God that we grudged nought
Upon this fair heath.
Isaac. Ah, father, I thank our Lord every deal, *unreservedly*
That my wit served me so well
410 For to dread God more than my death.

Abr. Why, dearworthy son, were thou adread?   *beloved*
Hardily, child, tell me thy lore.
Isaac. Yea, by my faith, father, now have I red
I was never so afraid before
415 As I have been at yon hill.
But, by my faith, father, I swear
I will nevermore come there
But it be against my will.

Abr. Yea, come on with me, my own sweet son,
420 And homeward fast now let us gon.   *go*
Isaac. By my faith, father, thereto I grant;   *agree*
I had never so good will to go home,
And to speak with my dear mother.
Abr. Ah, Lord of heaven, I thank thee,
425 For now may I lead home with me
Isaac, my young son so free,
The gentlest child above all other—
This may I well avow.

Now go we forth, my blessed son.
430 *Isaac.* I grant, father, and let us gon;

412 Tell me boldly, child, what you think.
413 Now I have thought.

For, by my troth, were I at home,
I would never for me out yonder gon.
I pray God give us grace evermo,   *evermore*
And all those that we be holden to.   *obliged*

[*Enter Doctor*]

435 *Doctor.*   Lo, sovereigns and sirs, now have we showed
    This solemn story to great and small.
    It is good learning to learned and lewd,   *ignorant*
    And the wisest of us all,
    Without any bering;
440 For this story showeth you here
    How we should keep, to our power,
    God's commandments without grudging.   *complaining*

    Trow ye, sirs, and God sent an angel,   *if*
    And commanded you your child to slain,   *slay*
445 By your troth, is there any of you
    That either would grudge or strive thereagain?   *against it*

    How think ye now, sirs, thereby?   *of that*
    I trow there be three or four or mo;
    And these women that weep so sorrowfully
450 When that their children die from fro,
    As nature will and kind.
    It is but folly, I may well avow,
    To grudge against God or to grieve you,
    For ye shall never see him mischiefed, well I know,   *harmed*
455 By land nor water.   Have this in mind,

    And grudge not against our Lord God,
    In wealth or woe, whether that   *happiness; whichever*
      he you send,
    Though ye be never so hard bested;
    For when he will, he may it amend,

439 Without any clamour, i.e. indisputably.
441 As far as we are able.
450-1 When their children die and leave them, as nature requires.

460   His commandments truly if ye keep with good
            heart,
        As this story hath now showed you beforn,   *before*
        And faithfully serve him while ye be quart,   *healthy*
        That ye may please God both even and morn.
        Now Jesus, that weareth the crown of thorn,
465   Bring us all to heaven's bliss.

THE COVENTRY PAGEANT OF THE
SHEARMEN AND TAILORS

THE ANNUNCIATION

The true Coventry cycle is represented by only two surviving pageants, which were once acted by the Shearmen and Tailors and by the Weavers of Coventry respectively. The following text is the first part (lines 1–203) of the pageant of the Shearmen and Tailors, and comprises a prologue by Isaiah, the Annunciation to Mary, the Doubt of Joseph, and the Journey to Bethlehem. It is immediately followed in the complete pageant of 900 lines by the Nativity and the Visit of the Shepherds. A dialogue between two unnamed Prophets then separates the above episodes from the rest of the pageant, which includes Herod and the Magi, the Magi at Bethlehem, the Flight to Egypt, and finally the Massacre of the Innocents.

Two interesting features of the part of the pageant given here are the prophetic prologue spoken by Isaiah and the Doubt of Joseph. The first of these is already found in embryo in an eleventh-century Christmas trope (see p. 79). It links up with the dialogue between the two unnamed Prophets later in the pageant, and it probably shows the influence of the liturgical Prophet plays and of the sixth-century sermon (*Sermo de Symbolo*) from which these plays are derived. The Doubt of Joseph (or Joseph's Trouble about Mary, as it is sometimes called) occurs in all the English cycles. There is very little biblical warrant for this episode, which may originally have been suggested by the apocryphal gospel known as Pseudo-Matthew, chapters x–xi. It certainly gave the medieval dramatist an opportunity for pathos and broad humour, and he did not fail to make the most of it.

We are dependent on Sharp's transcripts (published in 1817 and 1825) of the pageant of the Shearmen and Tailors, the manuscript of which was destroyed in the burning of the Free Reference Library at Birmingham in 1879. But a sixteenth-century manuscript containing the Weavers' pageant is still preserved and has been edited by Hardin Craig for the Early English Text Society. This manuscript is on deposit by its owners, the Broadweavers' and Clothiers' Company, in the City Archives at St Mary's Hall, Coventry.

THE ANNUNCIATION

[Isaiah's prophetic prologue]

Isaiah.   The Sovereign that seeth every secret,
    He save you all and make you perfect and sound,
    And give us grace with his mercy for to meet;
    For now in great misery mankind is bound:
5   The serpent hath given us so mortal a wound
    That no creature is able us for to release,
    Till thy right unction of Judah doth seize.

    Then shall much mirth and joy increase,
    And the right root in Israel spring,
10   That shall bring forth the grain of holiness;
    And out of danger he shall us bring
    Into that region where he is king,
    Which above all other far doth abound;
    And that cruel Satan he shall confound.

15   Wherefore I come here upon this ground   *earth*
    To comfort every creature of birth;   *who is born*
    For I, Isaiah the prophet, have found
    Many sweet matters whereof we may make mirth,
    On this same wise:
20   For though that Adam be deemed to death   *condemned*
    With all his children, as Abel and Seth,
    Yet *Ecce, virgo concipiet*—
    Lo, where a remedy shall rise!

    7 Till thy true unction (i.e. spiritual influence) takes possession of Judah.
    13 Which is far richer than all others.
    18–19 Many agreeable things at which we can rejoice, as thus.
    22 Behold, a virgin shall conceive.

Behold, a maiden shall conceive a child
25 And get us more grace than ever men had,
And her maidenhood nothing defiled; *in no way*
She is deputed to bear the Son, almighty God.
Lo, sovereigns, now may you be glad, *sirs*
For of this maiden all we may be fain;
30 For Adam, that now lies in sorrows full sad, *grievous*
His glorious birth shall redeem him again
From bondage and thrall. *servitude*
Now be merry, every man,
For this deed briefly in Israel shall be done, *soon*
35 And before the Father in throne,
That shall glad us all.

More of this matter fain would I move,
But longer time I have not here for to dwell.
That Lord that is merciful his mercy so in us **may**
    prove,
40 For to save our souls from the darkness of hell;
And to his bliss
He us bring,
As he is
Both Lord and King,
45 And shall be everlasting,
In saecula saeculorum. Amen.

[SCENE I. *The home of Mary*]

Gabriel. Hail, Mary, full of grace!
Our Lord God is with thee;
Above all women that ever was,
50 Lady, blessed mote thou be. *may*

Mary. Almighty Father and King of bliss,
From all disease thou save me now; *distress*
For inwardly my spirit troubled is,
That I am amazed and know not how. *confused*

35 And in the presence of the Father on His throne.
37 I would gladly say.
39 May the Lord who is merciful so evince in us His mercy.
46 For ever and ever.

55 *Gabr.*   Dread thee nothing, maiden, of this;
From heaven above hither am I sent
Of embassage from that King of bliss   *on a mission*
Unto thee, lady and virgin reverent,
Saluting thee here as most excellent,
60 Whose virtue above all doth abound;
Wherefore in thee grace shall be found,
For thou shalt conceive upon this ground
The Second Person of God in throne.
He will be born of thee alone,
65 Without sin thou shalt him see;
Thy grace and thy goodness will never be gone,
But ever to live in virginity.

Mary.   I marvel sore how that may be;
Man's company knew I never yet,
70 Nor never to do, cast I me,
While that our Lord sendeth me my wit.   *understanding*

Gabr.   The Holy Ghost in thee shall light,   *alight*
And shadow thy soul so with virtue
From the Father that is on height: *high*
75 These words, turtle, they be full true.

This child that of thee shall be born
Is the Second Person in Trinity:
He shall save that was forlorn,
And the fiend's power destroy shall he.

80 These words, lady, full true they been.
And further, lady, here in thine own lineage   *family*
Behold Elizabeth, thy cousin clean,   *pure*
The which was barren and past all age,

And now with child she hath been
85 Six months and more, as shall be seen;
Wherefore, discomfort thee not, Mary,
For to God impossible nothing may be.

70 And I resolve never to do so.
75 Turtle-dove (as a term of endearment).
78 Those who were damned.
83 i.e. past the age for bearing children.

Mary. Now, and it be that Lord's will   *if*
    Of my body to be born and for to be,   *live*
90   His high pleasures for to fulfil,
    As his own handmaid I submit me.

    Gabr. Now blessed be the time set   *appointed*
    That thou wast born in thy degree;
    For now is the knot surely knit,
95   And God conceived in Trinity.

    Now farewell, lady, of mights most:
    Unto the Godhead I thee beteach.   *commit*
    Mary. That Lord thee guide in every coast,
    And lowly he lead me and be my leech!   *saviour*

    Here the Angel departeth, and Joseph cometh in and
      saith :

100 *Joseph.* Mary, my wife so dear,
    How do ye, dame, and what cheer
    Is with you this tide?
    Mary. Truly, husband, I am here
    Our Lord's will for to abide.

105 *Jos.* What, I trow that we be all shent!   *believe; disgraced*
    Say, woman, who hath been here since I went,
    To rage with thee?   *behave wantonly*
    Mary. Sir, here was neither man nor man's even,   *likeness*
    But only the sond of our Lord God in heaven.   *messenger*
110 *Jos.* Say not so, woman; for shame, let be!   *leave off*

    Ye be with child so wondrous great,
    Ye need no more thereof to treat
    Against all right.
    Forsooth, this child, dame, is not mine.
115   Alas, that ever with mine eyne   *eyes*
    I should see this sight!

93 To thy [high] estate.
96 Of greatest power.
98 In every quarter, i.e. everywhere.
102 This time, i.e. now.
112 You need not argue about it any more.

Tell me, woman, whose is this child?

Mary.　None but yours, husband so mild,
　And that shall be seen, iwis.　　　　　　　*certainly*

120 *Jos.*　But mine?　Alas, alas, why say ye so?
　Welaway, woman, now may I go　　　　　　*alas*
　Beguiled, as many another is.

Mary.　Nay, truly, sir, ye be not beguiled,
　Nor yet with spot of sin I am defiled;

125 　Trust it well, husband.
Jos.　Husband, in faith, and that a-cold!
　Ah, welaway, Joseph, as thou art old!　　　*since*
　Like a fool now may I stand
　And truss.

130 　But, in faith, Mary, thou art in sin,
　So much as I have cherished thee, dame, and all
　　thy kin,
　Behind my back to serve me thus.

　All old men, example take by me—
　How I am beguiled here may you see—

135 　To wed so young a child.
　Now farewell, Mary, I leave thee here alone—
　Woe worth thee, dame, and thy works each one!—
　For I will no more be beguiled
　For friend nor foe.　　　　　　[*He leaves her.*

140 　Now of this deed I am so dull,
　And of my life I am so full,　　　　　　*weary*
　No farther may I go.

[*He lies down to rest, and an Angel says to him:*

Angel.　Arise up, Joseph, and go home again
　Unto Mary, thy wife, that is so free.　　　*noble*

145 　To comfort her look that thou be fain,
　For, Joseph, a clean maiden is she:

126 And a gloomy one!
128–9 Now may I stand and go like a fool, i.e. look a fool at all times.
131 Inasmuch as.
137 Bad luck to thee, wife, and all thy doings.
139 i.e. for anyone.
140 Now am I so downcast by this deed.

        She hath conceived without any train   *guile*
        The Second Person in Trinity;
        Jesus shall be his name, certain,   *assuredly*
150   And all this world save shall he;
        Be not aghast.   *afraid*
    Jos. Now, Lord, I thank thee with heart full sad, *steadfast*
        For of these tidings I am so glad
        That all my care away is cast;
155   Wherefore to Mary I will in haste.

                                    [*He returns to Mary.*

        Ah, Mary, Mary, I kneel full low;
        Forgive me, sweet wife, here in this land.
        Mercy, Mary, for now I know
        Of your good governance and how it doth stand.

160   Though that I did thee misname,   *abuse*
        Mercy, Mary! While I live
        Will I never, sweet wife, thee grieve
        In earnest nor in game.
    Mary. Now, that Lord in heaven, sir, he you forgive;
165   And I do forgive you in his name
        For evermore.
    Jos. Now truly, sweet wife, to you I say the same.

        But now to Bedlem must I wend   *Bethlehem*
        And show myself, so full of care.
170   Am I to leave you, thus great, behind?   *great with child*
        God wot, the while, dame, how you should fare.

    Mary. Nay, hardily, husband, dread ye nothing, *certainly*
        For I will walk with you on the way.
        I trust in God, almighty King,
175   To speed right well in our journey.

        159 Of your good behaviour and how matters stand.
        163 Seriously or jestingly, i.e. at all.
        171 God knows, wife, how you would fare the while.

Jos.   Now I thank you, Mary, of your goodness
 That ye my words will not blame;
 And since that to Bedlem we shall us dress, *must go*
 Go we together in God's holy name.

   [SCENE II. *The road to Bethlehem*]

180 Now to Bedlem have we leagues three;
 The day is nigh spent, it draweth toward night;
 Fain at your ease, dame, I would that ye should be,
 For you grow all weary, it seemeth in my sight.

 Mary.   God have mercy, Joseph, my spouse so dear;
185 All prophets hereto do bear witness,
 The very time now draweth near
 That my child will be born, which is King of bliss.

 Unto some place, Joseph, hendly me lead, *gently*
 That I might rest me with grace in this tide.
190 The light of the Father over us both spread,
 And the grace of my son with us here abide.

 Jos.   Lo, blessed Mary, here shall ye lend, *stay*
 Chief chosen of our Lord and cleanest in degree;
 And I for help to town will I wend.
195 Is not this the best, dame?   What say ye?

 Mary.   God have mercy, Joseph, my husband so meek;
 And heartily I pray you, go now from me. *earnestly*
 Jos.   That shall be done in haste, Mary so sweet;
 The comfort of the Holy Ghost leave I with thee.

200 Now to Bedlem straight will I wend
 To get some help for Mary so free;
 Some help of women God may me send,
 That Mary, full of grace, pleased may be.

  182 I would be glad, wife, if you were resting comfortably.
  190 May the light of the Father.
  193 The supreme chosen one of our Lord and the purest in state.

THE WAKEFIELD SECOND
SHEPHERDS' PAGEANT

The Shepherds' Plays in all the English cycles go back to a liturgical *Officium Pastorum*, which in turn grew out of a Latin Christmas trope. An idea of the evolution of this play during some four centuries can be got by comparing the early fifteenth-century *Second Shepherds' Pageant* with the following translation of an eleventh-century Christmas trope from Limoges (see Young, ii. 4), which is arranged as a dialogue between the shepherds and certain persons stationed at the manger:

'Whom do ye seek at the manger, shepherds? Speak!'

'Christ the Saviour, the infant Lord wrapped in swaddling-clothes, according to the words of the angel.'

'The child is here with Mary his mother, of whom long ago the prophet Isaiah spoke, prophesying: "Behold a virgin shall conceive and bear a son." And now as ye go forth say that he is born.'

'Alleluia, alleluia! Now do we know truly that Christ is born into the world; of whom let all sing, saying with the prophet:

Puer natus est.'

The *Second Shepherds' Pageant* in the Towneley cycle makes use of details taken from the second chapter of Luke and from the liturgical Christmas plays. But the playwright has humanized the shepherds and boldly combined the story of the Nativity with a pseudo-nativity involving a stolen sheep. He has borrowed the story of Mak the sheep-stealer from folklore (see Cosbey) and contrived to make a close-knit unity of his comic and serious scenes (see Watt).

It is not known which guild acted this pageant, but the Shepherds' Play was performed at York by the Chandlers and at Chester by the Painters and Glaziers, while at Coventry it formed part of the pageant of the Shearmen and Tailors. It is puzzling to find that the Towneley cycle includes two Shepherds' Plays, instead of a Nativity Play and a Shepherds' Play, as in the York and Chester cycles. Possibly the two Towneley plays were written for different guilds; possibly the author of the *First Shepherds' Pageant* realized that he could improve on his own handiwork, and did so in the pageant given here.

At least there need be no doubt that the two Shepherds' Plays in the Towneley cycle are by the same author, who lived in Wakefield or its neighbourhood. This outstanding playwright was also responsible for four more complete pageants (the *Murder of Abel*, *Noah and his Sons*, *Herod the Great*, and the *Buffeting*), as well as for parts of several others. The 'Wakefield Group,' as the Wakefield author's work is usually called, is distinguished from the rest of the cycle by its local allusions (e.g. to Horbury in the present pageant) and by its use of a nine-line stanza, with internal rhymes in the first four lines, to which no exact parallel has been found elsewhere. It is further distinguished by its lively exploitation of colloquial idiom and bold rehandling of secular material for comic purposes.

The whole Towneley cycle (so called because the manuscript was long in the possession of the Towneley family) is now believed by many scholars to be the Corpus Christi play of Wakefield, which the woollen industry made prosperous enough to support a full cycle of pageants by, at latest, the middle of the fifteenth century. The cycle has been edited by England and Pollard for the Early English Text Society. The following text is taken, with a few emendations, from photographs of the pageants in what is now Huntington Library MS. HM I. This manuscript, dating from the last decades of the fifteenth century, may once have been used as a municipal register of the pageants, like the manuscript containing the York cycle.

CHARACTERS

COLL   *the First Shepherd*

GIB   *the Second Shepherd*

DAW   *the Third Shepherd*

MAK   *the Sheep-stealer*

GILL   *Mak's Wife*

ANGEL

MARY   *with the Christ-child*

THE SECOND SHEPHERDS' PAGEANT

[SCENE I. *The open fields*]

1 Shepherd. Lord, what these weathers are cold!
  And I am ill happed.
I am near-hand dold, so long have I napped; *nearly numb*
My legs they fold, my fingers are chapped. *give way*
It is not as I would, for I am all lapped *wrapped*
5 In sorrow.
  In storms and tempest,
  Now in the east, now in the west,
  Woe is him has never rest
  Mid-day nor morrow!

10 But we sely husbands that walk on the moor,
  In faith, we are near-hands out of the door.
  No wonder, as it stands, if we be poor,
  For the tilth of our lands lies fallow as the floor,
  As ye ken.
15 We are so hammed, *crippled*
  Fortaxed and rammed, *overtaxed; crushed*
  We are made hand-tamed
  With these gentlery-men.

  Thus they reave us our rest, our Lady them wary!
20 These men that are lord-fast, they cause the plough
    tarry.
  That, men say, is for the best; we find it contrary.
  Thus are husbands oppressed, in point to miscarry
  On live.

1 How cold this weather is! And I am poorly clad.
10 But we poor husbandmen.
11 We are nearly homeless.
13 *tilth*, arable part.
17–18 We are reduced to submission by these gentry.
19 They rob us of our rest, our Lady curse them!
20 *lord-fast*, bound to a lord.
22–3 In danger of coming to mortal harm.

81

Thus hold they us under,
25   Thus they bring us in blunder;   *trouble*
It were great wonder
And ever should we thrive.   *if*

For may he get a paint sleeve or a brooch,
    nowadays,
Woe is him that him grieve, or once again-says!   *gainsays*
30   Dare no man him repreve, what mastery he mays;
And yet may no man lieve one word that he   *believe*
    says—
No letter.
He can make purveyance
With boast and bragance,   *bragging*
35   And all is through maintenance   *support*
Of men that are greater.

There shall come a swain as proud as a po;   *peacock*
He must borrow my wain, my plough also;
Then I am full fain to grant ere he go.
40   Thus live we in pain, anger, and woe
By night and day.
He must have, if he langed,
If I should forgang it;
I were better be hanged
45   Than once say him nay.

It does me good, as I walk thus by mine own,   *myself*
Of this world for to talk in manner of moan.   *grumble*
To my sheep will I stalk and harken anon,
There abide on a balk, or sit on a stone
50   Full soon;
For I trow, pardie,   *by God*
True men if they be,
We get more company
Ere it be noon.

28 If he is able to get an embroidered sleeve, i.e. a lord's livery.
30 No man dare reprove him, no matter what force he uses.
33 He can requisition [our belongings].
42–3 He must have what he wants, even if I have to go without it.
49 *balk*, a strip of rough grassland dividing two ploughed portions of
a common field.

[*Enter Second Shepherd*]

55 *2 Shep.* Benste and Dominus, what may this
        bemean?   *mean*
      Why fares this world thus?   Oft have we not seen.
      Lord, these weathers are spitous, and the winds   *cruel*
        full keen,
      And the frosts so hideous they water mine een—   *eyes*
      No lie.
60   Now in dry, now in wet,
      Now in snow, now in sleet,
      When my shoon freeze to my feet
      It is not all easy.

      But as far as I ken, or yet as I go,
65   We sely wedmen dree mickle woe:
      We have sorrow then and then; it falls oft so.
      Silly Copple, our hen, both to and fro
      She cackles;
      But begin she to croak,
70   To groan or to cluck,
      Woe is him our cock,
      For he is in the shackles.

      These men that are wed have not all their will;
      When they are full hard sted, they sigh full still.
75   God wot they are led full hard and full ill;
      In bower nor in bed they say nought theretill
      This tide.
      My part have I fun,
      I know my lesson:
80   Woe is him that is bun,   *bound* (*in marriage*)
      For he must abide.   *remain so*

55 *Benste*, benedicite (bless us).
56 We have not often seen the like.
64–6 But as far as I know or as my experience goes, we poor married
men suffer much woe: we have sorrow time and again.
71 Unhappy is our cock.
74 When they are hard put to it they sigh unceasingly.
76–8 They don't answer back now.   I've found out what I have to do.

But now late in our lives—a marvel to me,
That I think my heart rives such wonders to see;   *breaks*
What that destiny drives it should so be—
85   Some men will have two wives, and some men three
In store;
Some are woe that have any.   *miserable*
But so far can I: *know*
Woe is him that has many,
90   For he feels sore.   *pain*

But young men, of wooing, for God that you bought,
Be well ware of wedding, and think in your   *very wary*
    thought:
'Had I wist' is a thing that serveth of nought.
Mickle still mourning has wedding home brought,   *constant*
95   And griefs,
With many a sharp shower;   *pang*
For thou mayst catch in an hour
That shall sow thee full sour
As long as thou lives.

100   For, as ever read I epistle, I have one to my fere
As sharp as thistle, as rough as a briar.
She is browed like a bristle, with a sour-loten cheer;
Had she once wet her whistle, she could sing full
    clear
Her paternoster.
105   She is as great as a whale,
She has a gallon of gall;
By him that died for us all,
I would I had run to I had lost her!   *till*

84 Whatever destiny compels must come to pass.
91 But young men, as for wooing, by God who redeemed you.
93 'If only I had known' is something that doesn't help you.
98 What shall grieve you most bitterly.
100 I have one for my mate.
102 She has bristly brows and a sour-looking face.

   1 Shep.   God look over the raw!   Full deafly ye
     stand.
110 *2 Shep.*   Yea, the devil in thy maw, so tariand!
     Saw'st thou awre of Daw?
   1 Shep.   Yea, on a lea-land
     Heard I him blow.   He comes here at hand,
     Not far.
     Stand still.
   2 Shep.   Why?
115 *1 Shep.*   For he comes, hope I.   *think*
   2 Shep.   He will make us both a lie,   *tell*
     But if we beware.   *unless*

[Enter Third Shepherd]

   3 Shep.   Christ's cross me speed, and Saint Nicholas!
     Thereof had I need; it is worse than it was.
120 Whoso could take heed and let the world pass,
     It is ever in dread and brickle as glass,
     And slithes.
     This world fared never so,
     With marvels mo and mo—   *more*
125 Now in weal, now in woe,
     And all thing writhes.   *changes*

     Was never since Noah's flood such floods seen,
     Winds and rains so rude, and storms so keen:
     Some stammered, some stood in doubt, as I ween.   *fear*
130 Now God turn all to good!   I say as I mean,
     For ponder: *consider*
     These floods so they drown,

---

   109 God save the audience!   You stand there as deaf as a post.   (The
First Shepherd has evidently been trying to attract the other's attention.)
   110–12 The devil in your belly for tarrying so long!   Have you seen
Daw anywhere? . . . Yea, in a fallow field I heard him blow [his horn].
   119 *it*, i.e. the world.
   120–3 Anyone who could look on and let the world go by [would see
that] it is always fearful and as brittle as glass, and slides away (i.e. is
transitory).   The world never behaved in this way [before].

Both in fields and in town,
And bear all down;
135 And that is a wonder.

We that walk on the nights our cattle to keep,
We see sudden sights when other men sleep.
Yet methink my heart lights; I see   *grows light*
    shrews peep.   *rogues*
Ye are two all-wights! I will give my sheep   *monsters*
140 A turn.
But full ill have I meant;
As I walk on this bent,
I may lightly repent,
My toes if I spurn.

145 Ah, sir, God you save, and master mine!
A drink fain would I have, and somewhat to dine.
  1 Shep. Christ's curse, my knave, thou art a
    lither hine!   *lazy hind*
  2 Shep. What, the boy list rave! Abide unto syne;
  We have made it.
150 Ill thrift on thy pate!   *luck*
Though the shrew came late,
Yet is he in state   *ready*
To dine—if he had it.

  3 Shep. Such servants as I, that sweat and swinks,   *toil*
155 Eat our bread full dry, and that me forthinks. *displeases*
We are oft wet and weary when master-men winks; *sleep*
Yet come full lately both dinners and drinks.   *tardily*
But nately   *thoroughly*
Both our dame and our sire,
160 When we have run in the mire,
They can nip at our hire,
And pay us full lately.

139–44 I will turn my sheep round. But I have thought ill [of the shepherds]; as I walk in this field, I may soon feel sorry, if I stub my toes.
148–9 What, the boy is pleased to rave! Wait till later; we have finished it (i.e. our meal).
161 They can stint our wages.

But hear my truth, master: for the fare that ye make,
I shall do thereafter—work as I take.
165 I shall do a little, sir, and among ever lake,
For yet lay my supper never on my stomach
In fields.
Whereto should I threap?   *haggle*
With my staff can I leap;
170 And men say 'Light cheap
Litherly foryields.'

1 Shep.   Thou wert an ill lad to ride on wooing
With a man that had but little of spending.
2 Shep.   Peace, boy, I bade. No more jangling,
175 Or I shall make thee full rad, by the heaven's king!
With thy gauds—
Where are our sheep, boy?—we scorn.
3 Shep.   Sir, this same day at morn
I them left in the corn,
180 When they rang Lauds.

They have pasture good, they cannot go wrong.
1 Shep.   That is right. By the rood, these nights   *cross*
     are long!
Yet I would, ere we yode, one gave us a song.   *went*
2 Shep.   So I thought as I stood, to mirth us among.
185 *3 Shep.*   I grant.
1 Shep.   Let me sing the tenory.   *tenor*
2 Shep.   And I the treble so high.
3 Shep.   Then the mean falls to me.
Let see how ye chant.   [*They sing.*

163–5 But hear my promise, master: in return for the food you provide,
I shall do accordingly—work as I'm paid. I shall do but little, sir,
and betweenwhiles play all the time.

170–3 'A cheap bargain repays badly.' . . . You'd be the wrong lad for
anyone that's hard up to take a-wooing with him (cf. *Othello* III. iii. 71).

174–7 Stop your wrangling, or I'll quickly make you, by the king of
heaven! We scorn your pranks—where are our sheep, boy?

180 *Lauds*, the first of the seven canonical offices, usually sung at
daybreak.

184 To gladden us meanwhile.

Then Mak enters with a cloak covering his tunic.

190 *Mak.*   Now, Lord, for thy names seven, that made
           both moon and starns
       Well more than I can neven, thy will, Lord, of me
           tharns.
       I am all uneven; that moves oft my harns.
       Now would God I were in heaven, for there weep
           no bairns
       So still.   *incessantly*

195 *1 Shep.*   Who is that pipes so poor?
    Mak.   Would God ye wist how I foor!   *knew; fared*
       Lo, a man that walks on the moor,
       And has not all his will.

    2 Shep.   Mak, where hast thou gone?   Tell us
           tiding.   *news*
200 *3 Shep.*   Is he come?   Then ilkone take heed   *everyone*
           to his thing.

                   He takes Mak's cloak from him.

    Mak.   What! I be a yeoman, I tell you, of the king,
       The self and the same, sond from a great   *messenger*
           lording,
       And sich.   *suchlike*
       Fie on you!   Go hence
205   Out of my presence!
       I must have reverence.
       Why, who be ich?

    1 Shep.   Why make ye it so quaint?   Mak, ye do
           wrong.
    2 Shep.   But, Mak, list ye saint?   I trow that ye
           long.
210 *3 Shep.*   I trow the shrew can paint, the devil   *deceive*
           might him hang!

       190–2 Now, Lord, by thy seven names, who made both moon and stars
    far more than I can name, thy will concerning me, Lord, is lacking.   I am
    all at sixes and sevens; that often unsettles my brain.
       195 Who is it that cries so piteously?
       208 Why are you so uppish?
       209 But, Mak, do you want to play the saint?   I believe you do.

Mak.   I shall make complaint, and make you all **to**
   thwang
   At a word,
   And tell even how ye doth.   *do*
1 Shep.   But, Mak, is that sooth?
215   Now take out that Southern tooth,
   And set in a turd!   *put*

2 Shep.   Mak, the devil in your eye!   A stroke
   would I lene you.   *give*
3 Shep.   Mak, know ye not me?   By God, I
   could teen you.   *hurt*
Mak.   God look you all three!   Methought I   *save*
   had seen you.
220   Ye are a fair company.
1 Shep.   Can ye now mean you?
2 Shep.   Shrew, peep!   *pry about*
   Thus late as thou goes,
   What will men suppose?   *suspect*
   And thou hast an ill noise   *reputation*
225   Of stealing of sheep.   *for*

Mak.   And I am true as steel, all men wot;
   But a sickness I feel that holds me full hot: *severely*
   My belly fares not well, it is out of estate.   *condition*
3 Shep.   Seldom lies the devil dead by the gate.
230 *Mak.*   Therefore
   Full sore am I and ill;
   If I stand stone-still,
   I eat not a needle
   This month and more.

235 *1 Shep.*   How fares thy wife?   By my hood, how
   fares she?
Mak.   Lies waltering—by the rood—by the   *sprawling*
   fire, lo!

211 And have you all flogged.
215 Southern speech.   (Mak has been trying to talk Southern English.)
220 Can you remember now?
229 Seldom lies the devil dead by the roadside, i.e. appearances may be
deceptive.
232-3 As sure as I stand stone-still, I haven't eaten a morsel.

And a house full of brood.   She drinks well, too; *children*
Ill speed other good that she will do!
But she
240 Eats as fast as she can,
And ilk year that comes to man   *every*
She brings forth a lakan—   *baby*
And, some years, two.

But were I now more gracious, and richer   *prosperous*
      by far,
245 I were eaten out of house and of harbour.   *home*
Yet is she a foul dowse, if ye come near;   *wench*
There is none that trows nor knows a war
Than ken I.
Now will ye see what I proffer?
250 To give all in my coffer
To-morn at next to offer
Her head-masspenny.

   2 *Shep.*   I wot so forwaked is none in this shire;
I would sleep if I taked less to my hire.
255 3 *Shep.*   I am cold and naked, and would have a fire.
   1 *Shep.*   I am weary, forraked, and run in the mire—
Wake thou!
   2 *Shep.*   Nay, I will lie down by.   *near by*
For I must sleep, truly.
260 3 *Shep.*   As good a man's son was I
As any of you.

But, Mak, come hither!   Between shalt thou   *between us*
      lie down.
Mak.   Then might I let you bedene of that ye
      would rown,
No dread.

238 i.e. there is no hope of her doing much else.
247 There is none who believes [he knows] or [really] knows a worse one.
251-2 To-morrow at the latest to give all in my coffer as an offering for
her soul.
253 *forwaked*, wearied with waking.
254 Even if I should get less wages.
256 *forraked*, worn out with walking.
263-4 Then I might keep you from whispering what you want, no doubt.

265 From my top to my toe,   *[He recites a night-spell.*
    Manus tuas commendo,
    Pontio Pilato.
    Christ's cross me speed!

    Now were time for a man that lacks what he would,
270 To stalk privily then unto a fold,
    And nimbly to work then, and be not too bold,
    For he might abuy the bargain, if it were told
    At the ending.
    Now were time for to reel;   *move quickly*
275 But he needs good counsel
    That fain would fare well,
    And has but little spending.   *money*

    But about you a circle, as round as a moon,   *(magic) circle*
    To I have done what I will, till that it be noon,   *till*
280 That ye lie stone-still to that I have done;
    And I shall say theretill of good words a fone:
    'On height,   *high*
    Over your heads, my hand I lift.
    Out go your eyes! Fordo your sight!'
285 But yet I must make better shift,
    And it be right.

    Lord, what they sleep hard!—that may ye all hear.
    Was I never a shepherd, but now will I lere.   *learn*
    If the flock be scared, yet shall I nip near.
290 How! draw hitherward! Now mends our cheer
    From sorrow
    A fat sheep, I dare say,
    A good fleece, dare I lay.
    Eft-quit when I may,   *repay*
295 But this will I borrow.

               [He goes home with the sheep.

272–3 For he might pay dearly for it, if it came to a final reckoning.
281 And I shall also say a few good words.
284–7 'Perish your sight!' But yet I must make better efforts, if things are to come right. Lord, how soundly they sleep!
289 Yet I shall grab [a sheep] tightly.
290–2 Now a fat sheep shall comfort us.

[SCENE II. *Mak's cottage*]

Mak. How, Gill, art thou in? Get us some light.
Wife. Who makes such din this time of the night?
 I am set for to spin; I hope not I might
 Rise a penny to win, I shrew them on height!
300 So fares
 A housewife that has been,
 To be raised thus between.
 Here may no note be seen
 For such small chares.

305 *Mak.* Good wife, open the heck! See'st   *inner door*
 thou not what I bring?
Wife. I may thole thee draw the sneck. Ah,
 come in, my sweeting!
Mak. Yea, thou thar not reck of my long standing.
Wife. By the naked neck art thou like for to hang.
Mak. Do way!   *enough!*
310 I am worthy my meat,   *food*
 For in a strait can I get   *fix*
 More than they that swink and sweat   *toil*
 All the long day.

 Thus it fell to my lot, Gill; I had such grace.
315 *Wife.* It were a foul blot to be hanged for the case. *deed*
Mak. I have scaped, Jelott, oft as hard a glase. *blow*
Wife. 'But so long goes the pot to the water,' men
 says,
 'At last
 Comes it home broken.'
320 *Mak.* Well know I the token,   *portent*
 But let it never be spoken!
 But come and help fast.

298–304 I don't think I can earn a penny by getting up [from my spinning], curse them! Any woman who has been a housewife knows what it means to be got up from her work continually. I have no work to show because of such small chores.
306 I will let you draw the latch.
307 You needn't mind about my standing [outside] so long.

I would he were flain; I list well eat.
This twelvemonth was I not so fain of one sheep-
    meat.

325 *Wife.*   Come they ere he be slain, and hear the sheep
    bleat—

Mak.   Then might I be ta'en: that were a cold sweat!
    Go spar   *fasten*
    The gate-door.   *outer door*

Wife.   Yes, Mak,
    For and they come at thy back—   *if*

330 *Mak.*   Then might I buy, for all the pack,
    The devil of the war.

Wife.   A good bourd have I spied, since thou   *jest*
    canst none: *knowest*
    Here shall we him hide, till they be gone,
    In my cradle. Abide! Let me alone,
335   And I shall lie beside in childbed and groan.

Mak.   Thou red,   *get ready*
    And I shall say thou wast light   *delivered*
    Of a knave-child this night.   *boy*

Wife.   Now well is me day bright,
340   That ever was I bred!

This is a good guise and a far cast;
Yet a woman's advice helps at the last.
I wot never who spies; again go thou fast.

Mak.   But I come ere they rise, else blows a cold   *unless*
    blast!
345   I will go sleep.
    Yet sleep all this meny;   *company*
    And I shall go stalk privily,
    As it had never been I
    That carried their sheep.

323–4 I wish he were skinned; I am eager to eat. At no time this year
have I been so glad of a meal of mutton.
   330–1 Then I may get the devil of a bad time from the whole pack of
them.
   339–41 I 'm happy when I think of the bright day I was born! This is
a good method and a cunning trick.
   343 Return again quickly [to the others].

[SCENE III.   *The open fields*]

350 *1 Shep.*   *Resurrex a mortruus!* have hold my hand!
       Judas carnas dominus!   I may not well stand:
       My foot sleeps, by Jesus, and I walter fastand.
       I thought that we laid us full near England.
    2 Shep.   Ah, yea?   *oh, really*
355   Lord, what I have slept well!
       As fresh as an eel,
       As light I me feel
       As leaf on a tree.

    3 Shep.   Beriste be herein!   So me quakes,   *blessing*
360   My heart is out of skin, what-so it makes.
       Who makes all this din?   So my brow blakes,
       To the door will I win.   Hark, fellows,   *go*
          wakes!   *wake up*
       We were four:
       See ye awre of Mak now?
365 *1 Shep.*   We were up ere thou.
    2 Shep.   Man, I give God avow
       Yet yede he nawre.

    3 Shep.   Methought he was lapped in a wolf-skin.
    1 Shep.   So are many happed now—namely within.
370 *3 Shep.*   When we had long napped, methought with
          a gin   *snare*
       A fat sheep he trapped; but he made no din.
    2 Shep.   Be still!
       Thy dream makes thee wood;   *mad*
       It is but phantom, by the rood.
375 *1 Shep.*   Now God turn all to good,
       If it be his will.

          352 I'm tottering with hunger.
          355 How well I have slept!
          359-60 I tremble so much, my heart is in my mouth, whatever the
       reason for it.
          361 My brow darkens so [with fear].
          364 Have you seen Mak anywhere?
          366-7 I vow to God he's gone nowhere yet.
          369 Many are covered like that nowadays—especially on the inside.

2 *Shep.*   Rise, Mak, for shame!   Thou liest right long.
Mak.   Now Christ's holy name be us among!
    What is this?   For Saint Jame, I may not well
        gang!   *walk*
380   I trow I be the same.   Ah, my neck has lain wrong
    Enough.   [*They help him to get up.*
    Mickle thank!   Since yester-even,
    Now by Saint Stephen,
    I was flayed with a sweven—
385   My heart out of slough.

    I thought Gill began to croak and travail full sad,   *hard*
    Well-nigh at the first cock, of a young lad
    For to mend our flock.   Then be I never glad;   *increase*
    I have tow on my rock more than ever I had.
390   Ah, my head!
    A house full of young tharms,   *bellies*
    The devil knock out their harns!   *brains*
    Woe is him has many bairns,
    And thereto little bread.

395   I must go home, by your leave, to Gill, as I
        thought.   *intended*
    I pray you look my sleeve, that I steal nought;   *examine*
    I am loath you to grieve or from you take aught.
    3 *Shep.*   Go forth, ill might thou chieve!   Now   *prosper*
        would I we sought,
    This morn,
400   That we had all our store.
    1 Shep.   But I will go before.
    Let us meet.
    2 *Shep.*   Where?
    3 *Shep.*   At the crooked thorn.

379 By Saint James.
  380-1 I suppose I'm the same [man I was].   Ah, my neck has been
lying very crookedly.
  384-5 I was terrified by a dream—I nearly jumped out of my skin.
  389 I have more tow on my distaff (i.e. more trouble in store) than
ever I had.
  398–400 Now I want us this morning to see that we have all our stock.

[SCENE IV. *Mak's cottage*]

Mak.   Undo this door! Who is here? How long
       shall I stand?

405 *Wife.*   Who makes such a bere? Now walk in the   *din*
       wenyand!

Mak.   Ah, Gill, what cheer? It is I, Mak, your
       husband.

Wife.   Then may we see here the devil in a band,   *noose*
       Sir Guile!

       Lo, he comes with a lote,   *noise*

410   As he were holden in the throat.   *held by*

       I may not sit at my note   *work*

       A hand-long while.   *brief*

Mak.   Will ye hear what fare she makes to get her a
       glose?

       And does naught but lakes, and claws her toes.   *play*

415 *Wife.*   Why, who wanders, who wakes? Who comes,
       who goes?

       Who brews, who bakes? What makes me thus
       hoarse?

       And then

       It is ruth to behold—   *a pity*

       Now in hot, now in cold,

420   Full woeful is the household

       That wants a woman.   *lacks*

       But what end hast thou made with the herds,   *shepherds*
       Mak?

Mak.   The last word that they said when I turned
       my back,

       They would look that they had their sheep, all the
       pack.

425   I hope they will not be well paid when they   *think; pleased*
       their sheep lack,

       Pardie!

     405 Confound you! (The waning moon was considered an unlucky
time.)
     413 Will you listen to the fuss she makes to find deceitful words [in
order to win sympathy].
     419 i.e. at all times.

But how-so the game goes,   *however*
To me they will suppose,
And make a foul noise,
430 And cry out upon me.

But thou must do as thou hight.   *promised*
Wife.   I accord me theretill;
I shall swaddle him right in my cradle.
If it were a greater sleight, yet could I help till.   *trick*
I will lie down straight. Come hap me. *straightway; cover*
Mak.   I will.
435 *Wife.* Behind!
Come Coll and his marrow,   *mate*
They will nip us full narrow.   *hard*
Mak. But I may cry 'Out, harrow!'
The sheep if they find.

440 *Wife.* Harken ay when they call; they will come anon.
Come and make ready all, and sing by thine own;
Sing lullay thou shall, for I must groan,   *lullaby*
And cry out by the wall on Mary and John,
For sore.   *pain*
445 Sing lullay on fast,   *quickly*
When thou hearest at the last;
And but I play a false cast,
Trust me no more.

[SCENE V. *The crooked thorn*]

3 Shep. Ah, Coll, good morn! Why sleepest thou not?
450 *1 Shep.* Alas, that ever was I born! We have a foul blot—
A fat wether have we lorn.   *lost*
3 Shep.   Marry, God's forbot! *God forbid*
2 Shep. Who should do us that scorn? That were   *insult*
a foul spot.   *disgrace*
1 Shep. Some shrew.

428 They will suspect me.
431 I agree to that.
433 I could still help with it.
438 A cry for help.
447 And if I don't play a false trick.

I have sought with my dogs
455   All Horbury shrogs,   *thickets*
And, of fifteen hogs,
Found I but one ewe.

3 Shep.   Now trow me, if ye will—by Saint Thomas
of Kent,
Either Mak or Gill was at that assent.
460 *1 Shep.*   Peace, man, be still!   I saw when he went.
Thou slander'st him ill; thou ought to repent
Good speed.   *quickly*
2 Shep.   Now as ever might I thee,
If I should even here die,
465   I would say it were he
That did that same deed.

3 Shep.   Go we thither, I rede, and run on our feet.   *advise*
Shall I never eat bread, the sooth to I wit.
1 Shep.   Nor drink in my head, with him till I meet.
470 *2 Shep.*   I will rest in no stead till that I him greet,   *place*
My brother.
One I will hight:
Till I see him in sight,
Shall I never sleep one night
475   There I do another.   *where*

[SCENE VI.   *Mak's cottage*]

3 Shep.   Will ye hear how they hack?   Our sire
list croon.
1 Shep.   Heard I never none crack so clear out of   *sing*
tone.   *tune*
Call on him.
2 Shep.   Mak, undo your door soon!   *immediately*

455 Horbury, near Wakefield.
458 St Thomas of Canterbury.
456–7 Among fifteen hogs (or young sheep) I found only a ewe, i.e.
the wether was missing.
459 Either Mak or Gill was a party to it.
463 As I hope to prosper.
468 Till I know the truth.
471 *My brother*, a friendly form of address.
472 One thing I will promise.
476 Do you hear them trilling?   Our gentleman is pleased to croon.

Mak. Who is it that spake, as it were noon,
480   On loft?
   Who is that, I say?
3 Shep. Good fellows, were it day.   *if only it were*
Mak. As far as ye may,
   Good, speak soft,   *good sirs*

485 Over a sick woman's head, that is at maleease;
   I had liefer be dead ere she had any disease.
Wife. Go to another stead! I may not well quease; *breathe*
   Each foot that ye tread goes thorough my nose
   So high.
490 *1 Shep.* Tell us, Mak, if ye may,
   How fare ye, I say?
Mak. But are ye in this town to-day?
   Now how fare ye?

   Ye have run in the mire, and are wet yet;
495 I shall make you a fire, if ye will sit.
   A nurse would I hire. Think ye on yet?
   Well quit is my hire—my dream, this is it—
   A season.
   I have bairns, if ye knew,
500 Well more than enew;   *enough*
   But we must drink as we brew,
   And that is but reason.

   I would ye dined ere ye yode. Methink that ye   *went*
      sweat.
2 Shep. Nay, neither mends our mood drink nor meat.
505 *Mak.* Why, sir, ails you aught but good?
3 Shep.   Yea, our sheep that we gete   *tend*
   Are stolen as they yode. Our loss is great.
Mak. Sirs, drink!

479–80 Who is it that spoke aloud, as though it were noon?
485–6 Because of a sick woman who is in distress; I had rather die than
she should suffer any discomfort.
488–9 Every step you tread goes through my nose so strongly, i.e. goes
right through my head.
496–8 I would like to hire a nurse. Do you still remember [my dream
about a new addition to the family]? I 've been paid my wages in full
for a while—this is my dream come true.
505 Why, sir, is anything wrong with you?

Had I been there,
Some should have bought it full sore.   *paid for*

510 *1 Shep.*   Marry, some men trow that ye were,
And that us forthinks.   *displeases*

2 Shep.   Mak, some men trows that it should be ye.   *believe*
3 Shep.   Either ye or your spouse, so say we.
Mak.   Now if ye have suspose to Gill or to me,   *suspicion*
515 Come and rip our house, and then may ye see   *ransack*
Who had her.
If I any sheep fot,   *fetched*
Either cow or stot—   *heifer*
And Gill, my wife, rose not
520 Here since she laid her—

As I am true and leal, to God here I pray   *honest*
That this be the first meal that I shall eat this day.
1 Shep.   Mak, as have I sele, advise thee, I say:
He learned timely to steal that could not say nay.
525 *Wife.*   I swelt!   *feel faint*
Out, thieves, from my wones!   *house*
Ye come to rob us for the nonce.
Mak.   Hear ye not how she groans?
Your hearts should melt.

530 *Wife.*   Out, thieves, from my bairn!   Nigh him
not there.
Mak.   Wist ye how she had farn, your hearts would
be sore.
Ye do wrong, I you warn, that thus come before
To a woman that has farn; but I say no more.
Wife.   Ah, my middle!
535 I pray to God so mild,
If ever I you beguiled,
That I eat this child   *may eat*
That lies in this cradle.

523–4 Mak, as I hope for happiness, take thought I say: he learned early
to steal who could not say no.
527 You come on purpose to rob us.
530 Do not go near him there.
531 If you knew what she had been through.
533 To a woman who has been in labour.

Mak.   Peace, woman, for God's pain, and cry not so!

540   Thou spillest thy brain, and makest me full woe.   *injurest*

2 *Shep.*   I trow our sheep be slain.   What find ye two?

3 *Shep.*   All work we in vain; as well may we go. But hatters!   *confound it*

I can find no flesh,

545   Hard nor nesh,   *soft*

Salt nor fresh,

But two tome platters.   *only; empty*

Quick cattle but this, tame nor wild,

None, as have I bliss, as loud as he smelled.

550 *Wife.*   No, so God me bless, and give me joy of my child!

1 *Shep.*   We have marked amiss; I hold us beguiled.

2 *Shep.*   Sir, don.   *completely*

Sir—our Lady him save!—

Is your child a knave?   *boy*

555 *Mak.*   Any lord might him have,

This child, to his son.

When he wakens he kips, that joy is to see.   *snatches*

3 *Shep.*   In good time to his hips, and in sely.

But who were his gossips so soon ready?   *godparents*

560 *Mak.*   So fair fall their lips!

1 *Shep.*   [*Aside*]   Hark now, a lie!

Mak.   So God them thank,

Parkin, and Gibbon Waller, I say,

And gentle John Horne, in good fay—   *faith*

He made all the garray—   *commotion*

565   With the great shank.   *long legs*

548–9 Except for this (i.e. the 'baby' in the cradle), no livestock, tame or wild, as I hope to be happy, smelled as loud as he (i.e. the missing sheep).

551 We have made a mistake; I think we're deceived.

558 A good and happy future to him.

560 Good luck to them.

563 *John Horne* is the shepherd in the *First Shepherds' Pageant* who quarrels with Gyb about the pasturing of an imaginary flock of sheep.

2 Shep. Mak, friends will we be, for we are all one.   *agreed*
Mak. We? Now I hold for me, for mends get I
   none.
   Farewell all three!—all glad were ye gone.
3 Shep. Fair words may there be, but love is there
   none
570 This year.   [*They leave the cottage.*
1 Shep. Gave ye the child anything?
2 Shep. I trow not one farthing.
3 Shep. Fast again will I fling;
   Abide ye me there.   [*He returns to the cottage.*

575 Mak, take it to no grief, if I come to thy bairn.
Mak. Nay, thou dost me great reprief, and foul hast
   thou farn.
3 Shep. The child will it not grieve, that little
   day-starn.   *star*
   Mak, with your leave, let me give your bairn
   But sixpence.
580 *Mak.* Nay, do way! He sleeps.
3 Shep. Methink he peeps.
Mak. When he wakens he weeps.
   I pray you go hence.

3 Shep. Give me leave him to kiss, and lift up the
   clout.   [*He glimpses the sheep.*   *cloth*
585 What the devil is this? He has a long snout!
1 Shep. He is marked amiss. We wait ill about.
2 Shep. Ill-spun weft, iwis, ay comes foul out.
   Aye, so!   [*He recognizes the sheep.*
   He is like to our sheep!

    567 I take my own part, for I get no amends.
    568 [I should be] very glad if you were gone.   (Probably an aside.)
    573 I will dash back.
    575 Don't take offence.
    576 Nay, you do me great shame, and you have behaved badly.
    586–7 He is misshapen. We do wrong to pry about. . . . Ill-spun
weft, indeed, always comes out badly, i.e. what is bred in the bone will
come out in the flesh.

590   *3 Shep.*   How, Gib, may I peep?
      1 Shep.   I trow kind will creep
          Where it may not go.

      2 Shep.   This was a quaint gaud and a far cast;
          It was a high fraud.
      3 Shep.   Yea, sirs, was't.
595   Let burn this bawd and bind her fast.
      A false scold hangs at the last;
      So shalt thou.
      Will ye see how they swaddle
      His four feet in the middle?
600   Saw I never in a cradle
      A horned lad ere now.

      Mak.   Peace, bid I. What, let be your fare!   *uproar*
      I am he that him begat, and yond woman him bare.
      1 Shep.   What devil shall he hat, Mak?   Lo,   *be called*
          God, Mak's heir!
605 *2 Shep.*   Let be all that. Now God give him care,   *sorrow*
      I sagh.
      Wife.   A pretty child is he
      As sits on a woman's knee;
      A dillydown, pardie,   *darling*
610   To gar a man laugh.   *make*

      3 Shep.   I know him by the ear-mark; that is a good
          token.
      Mak.   I tell you, sirs, hark! his nose was broken.
      Since told me a clerk that he was forspoken.   *bewitched*
      1 Shep.   This is a false work; I would fain be   *avenged*
      wroken.
615   Get weapon!
      Wife.   He was taken with an elf,   *by*
      I saw it myself;
      When the clock struck twelve,
      Was he forshapen.   *transformed*

591–3 Nature will creep where it cannot walk, i.e. assert itself in one way or another. . . . This was a clever dodge and a cunning trick.
606 I saw [the sheep myself].

620 *2 Shep.*   Ye two are well feft sam in a stead.
 1 Shep.   Since they maintain their theft, let do them   *death*
  to dead.
 Mak.   If I trespass eft, gird off my head.   *again; strike*
  With you will I be left.
 3 Shep.   Sirs, do my rede:
  For this trespass
625 We will neither ban ne flite,   *curse; quarrel*
  Fight nor chide,
  But have done as tite,   *at once*
  And cast him in canvas.

      [*They toss Mak in a blanket.*

    [SCENE VII. *The open fields*]

 1 Shep.   Lord, what I am sore, in point for to burst!
630 In faith, I may no more; therefore will I rest.
 2 Shep.   As a sheep of seven score he weighed in my
  fist.
  For to sleep aywhere methink that I list.
 3 Shep.   Now I pray you
  Lie down on this green.
635 *1 Shep.*   On these thieves yet I mean.   *think*
 3 Shep.   Whereto should ye teen?   *vex yourself*
  Do as I say you.

  An Angel sings 'Gloria in excelsis,' and then says:

 Angel.   Rise, herdmen hend, for now is he born   *gentle*
  That shall take from the fiend that Adam had lorn;
640 That warlock to shend, this night is he born.   *destroy*
  God is made your friend now at this morn,
  He behests.   *promises*
  At Bedlem go see   *Bethlehem*
  There lies that free   *where; noble one*
645 In a crib full poorly,
  Betwixt two beasts.

  620 You two are well endowed together with a place, i.e. are in a fine fix.
  623 I want to be spared by you. . . .   Sirs, take my advice.
  632 I think I would be glad to sleep anywhere.
  640 *warlock,* the devil.

1 Shep.   This was a quaint steven that   *elegant voice*
    ever yet I heard.
    It is a marvel to neven, thus to be scared.   *tell of*
2 Shep.   Of God's son of heaven he spoke upward.   *on high*
650 All the wood on a leven methought that he gard
    Appear.
3 Shep.   He spake of a bairn
    In Bedlem, I you warn.
1 Shep.   That betokens yond starn;
655 Let us seek him there.

2 Shep.   Say, what was his song?   Heard ye not how
    he cracked it,   *sang*
    Three breves to a long?
3 Shep.   Yea, marry, he hacked it: *trilled*
    Was no crochet wrong, nor no thing that lacked it.
1 Shep.   For to sing us among, right as he
    knacked it,   *sang*
660 I can.
2 Shep.   Let see how ye croon.
    Can ye bark at the moon?
3 Shep.   Hold your tongues!   Have done!
1 Shep.   Hark after, then.   [*Sings.*

665 *2 Shep.*   To Bedlem he bade that we should gang;   *go*
    I am full adrad that we tarry too long.   *afraid*
3 Shep.   Be merry and not sad—of mirth is our song!
    Everlasting glad to meed may we fang
    Without noise.
670 *1 Shep.*   Hie we thither forthy,   *therefore*
    If we be wet and weary,   *even if*
    To that child and that lady;
    We have it not to lose.

650–1 I thought he made the whole wood appear as if lit up by lightning.
658 No crochet was wrong, and there was nothing it lacked.
668–9 We can get everlasting joy as our reward without any fuss.
673 We must not forget it.

2 Shep.   We find by the prophecy—let be your din!—

675   Of David and Isay, and more than I   *Isaiah*
    min—   *remember*
    They prophesied by clergy—that in a virgin   *learning*
    Should he light and lie, to sloken our sin,   *alight; quench*
    And slake it,   *relieve*
    Our kind, from woe;   *race*
680   For Isay said so:
    Ecce virgo
    Concipiet a child that is naked.

3 Shep.   Full glad may we be, and abide that day
    That lovely to see, that all mights may.
685   Lord, well were me for once and for ay,
    Might I kneel on my knee, some word for to say
    To that child.
    But the angel said
    In a crib was he laid;
690   He was poorly arrayed,
    Both meek and mild.

1 Shep.   Patriarchs that have been, and prophets
    beforn,   *in the past*
    They desired to have seen this child that is born.
    They are gone full clean; that have they lorn.
695   We shall see him, I ween, ere it be morn,
    To token.   *as a sign*
    When I see him and feel,
    Then wot I full well
    It is true as steel
700   That prophets have spoken:

    To so poor as we are that he would appear,
    First find, and declare by his messenger.
2 Shep.   Go we now, let us fare; the place is us near.

681–2 Behold, a virgin shall conceive.
684–5 To see that lovely one who is almighty.   Lord, I would be happy
for once and all.
694 That chance have they lost.
702 Find [us] first of all, and make known [his birth] through his
messenger.

   3 Shep. I am ready and yare; go we in fere   *eager; together*
705 To that bright.   *bright one*
      Lord, if thy will be—
      We are lewd all three—   *simple*
      Thou grant us some kins glee
      To comfort thy wight.

[SCENE VIII.   *The stable in Bethlehem*]

710 *1 Shep.* Hail, comely and clean; hail, young child!   *pure*
      Hail, maker, as I mean, of a maiden so mild!   *born of*
      Thou hast waried, I ween, the warlock so wild: *cursed*
      The false guiler of teen, now goes he beguiled.
      Lo, he merries,   *is merry*
715 Lo, he laughs, my sweeting!
      A well fare meeting!   *very fortunate*
      I have holden my heting:
      Have a bob of cherries.   *bunch*

   2 Shep. Hail, sovereign saviour, for thou hast us
         sought!
720 Hail, freely food and flower, that all thing hast *noble child*
         wrought!
      Hail, full of favour, that made all of nought!
      Hail!   I kneel and I cower.   A bird have I brought
      To my bairn.
      Hail, little tiny mop!   *moppet*
725 Of our creed thou art crop;
      I would drink on thy cop,
      Little day-starn.

   3 Shep. Hail, darling dear, full of Godhead!
      I pray thee be near when that I have need.
730 Hail, sweet is thy cheer!   My heart would bleed
      To see thee sit here in so poor weed,   *clothing*
      With no pennies.

708–9 Grant us some joyful way of comforting thy child.
713 The false and malicious deceiver, i.e. the devil.
717 I have kept my promise.
725–6 You are the head of our faith; I would drink in your cup (i.e.
the cup of the eucharist).

Hail!   Put forth thy dall!   *hand*
I bring thee but a ball:
735   Have and play thee withal,
And go to the tennis.

Mary.   The Father of heaven, God omnipotent,
That set all on seven, his Son has he sent.
My name could he neven, and light ere he went.
740   I conceived him full even through might, as he
meant;
And now is he born.
He keep you from woe!—
I shall pray him so.
Tell forth as ye go,
745   And min on this morn.   *remember*

1 Shep.   Farewell, lady, so fair to behold,
With thy child on thy knee.
2 Shep.   But he lies full cold.
Lord, well is me!   Now we go, thou behold.
3 Shep.   Forsooth, already it seems to be told
750   Full oft.
1 Shep.   What grace we have fun!
2 Shep.   Come forth; now are we won!   *redeemed*
3 Shep.   To sing are we bun: *bound*
Let take on loft.

738 That made all the world in seven days.
739-40 He named my name and alighted in me before He went. I
conceived him indeed through God's might, as His purpose was.
754 Let us begin loudly.

THE WAKEFIELD PAGEANT
OF
HEROD THE GREAT

Some of the features of this pageant and of its counterpart in the other English cycles are derived from scenes dramatizing the Slaughter of the Innocents in liturgical Magi plays. Thus Herod's *armati* in the *Officium Stellae* from Laon (see Young, ii. 105) are the prototypes of the soldiers in *Herod the Great*, while the attempted intervention of the mothers in the Fleury *Ordo Rachelis* (Young, ii. 111) foreshadows the episode of the three mothers in the present pageant. Above all, the tradition of the raging Herod (started by Matt. ii. 16) is emphasized in the liturgical plays.

The Wakefield playwright's skill in characterization is nowhere better shown than in this pageant. The ranting Herod of medieval tradition is re-created as a contemporary magnate. He graciously offers *grith* to those barons who will pay him homage. In his imagination the three kings of the Epiphany are planning an alliance with Christ which may result in his own downfall. He lives in a world of intrigue and counter-intrigue, of ruthless means and bloody ends. And his fear, greed, and anger find their natural outlet in verbal violence and abuse. To a fifteenth-century audience he would certainly have suggested a latter-day tyrant like the Duke of Suffolk, whose choleric behaviour in a court of law is compared with that of Herod, in a letter written to Sir John Paston in 1478: 'There was never no man that played Herod in Corpus Christi play better and more agreeable to his pageant than he [Suffolk] did' (*Paston Letters*, ed. N. Davis, ii. 426).

Apart from the Herod pageants in the English cycles, there is a fifteenth-century play on the Slaughter of the Innocents preserved in Bodley MS. Digby 133 (ed. Furnivall).

CHARACTERS

MESSENGER	THREE SOLDIERS
HEROD	THREE WOMEN
	TWO COUNSELLORS

HEROD THE GREAT

[SCENE I. *Before Herod's palace*]

Messenger. Most mighty Mahoun meng you with
    mirth!
    Both of burgh and of town, by fells and by firth,
    Both king with crown and barons of birth,
    That radly will rown, many great grith

5   Shall behap.
    Take tenderly intent   *carefully; heed*
    What sonds are sent,   *messages*
    Else harms shall ye hent,   *get*
    And loaths you to lap.

10   Herod, the hend king—by grace of Mahoun—   *gracious*
    Of Jewry, surmounting sternly with crown   *surpassing*
    On life that are living in tower and in town,
    Gracious you greeting, commands you be boun   *ready*
    At his bidding.

15   Love him with lewty;   *loyalty*
    Dread him, that doughty!
    He charges you be ready
    Lowly at his liking.   *pleasure*

    What man upon mold means him again,
20   Tite teen shall be told, knight, squire, or swain;
    Be he never so bold, buys he that bargain
    Twelve thousandfold more than I sayn,
    May ye trust.

1–5 Most mighty Mahomet make you merry! His great protection
shall be given to those burghers and country-folk, kings and barons of
noble birth, who will promptly speak in a whisper. (The Messenger is
asking the audience to be silent.)
   9 And troubles shall entangle you.
   12 Those who are living.
   19–23 Whoever on earth—knight, squire, or swain—speaks against
him shall quickly be considered troublesome; be he never so bold, rely
upon it, he shall pay a penalty twelve thousand times worse than I say.

He is worthy wonderly,	*wonderfully worthy*
25 Selcouthly sorry:	*strangely sad*
For a boy that is born hereby	
Stands he abashed.	*troubled*

A king they him call, and that we deny;	
How should it so fall, great marvel have I;	*happen*
30 Therefore overall shall I make a cry	
That ye busk not to brawl, nor like not to lie	*prepare*
This tide.	
Carp of no king	*speak*
But Herod, that lording,	
35 Or busk to your building,	*hurry; dwelling*
Your heads for to hide.	

He is king of kings, kindly I know,	*thoroughly*
Chief lord of lordings, chief leader of law.	
There wait on his wings that bold boast will blow;	
40 Great dukes down dings for his great awe	
And him lowt;	
Tuscany and Turkey,	
All India and Italy,	
Sicily and Surry	*Syria*
45 Dread him and doubt.	*fear*

From Paradise to Padua, to Mount Flascon,	
From Egypt to Mantua, unto Kemp town,	
From Sarceny to Susa, to Greece it abown,	*above it*
Both Normandy and Norway lowt to his crown.	*bow down*
50 His renown	
Can no tongue tell,	
From heaven unto hell;	
Of him can none spell	*speak*
But his cousin Mahoun.	

30 Therefore everywhere shall I make proclamation.
39–41 There are at his beck and call those who will boldly boast; great dukes fall down in great fear of him and reverence him.

55   He is the worthiest of all bairns that are born;
      Free men are his thrall, full teenfully torn.
      Begin he to brawl, many men catch scorn;   *if he begins*
      Obey must we all, or else be ye lorn   *lost*
      At once.
60   Down ding of your knees,
      All that him sees;
      Displeased he bese,   *shall be*
      And break many bones.

      Here he comes now, I cry, that lord I of spake!
65   Fast afore will I hie, radly on a rake,
      And welcome him worshipfully, laughing with lake,   *joy*
      As he is most worthy, and kneel for his sake
      So low;
      Down derfly to fall,   *promptly*
70   As rink most royal.
      Hail, the worthiest of all!
      To thee must I bow.

                         [*Enter Herod*]

      Hail, lief lord!   Lo, thy letters have I laid;   *beloved*
      I have done I could do, and peace have I prayed;
75   Mickle more thereto openly displayed.   *also*
      But rumour is raised so, that boldly they brade
      Among them:
      They carp of a king;
      They cease not such chattering.
80 *Herod.*   But I shall tame their talking,
      And let them go hang them.

      56 Free men are his vassals, most grievously injured.
      60 Force down your knees.
      65 Quickly running.
      70 As he is the most royal of men.
      73-4 I have presented your letter (*letters*=*sonds* in first stanza); I have
   done what I could do.
      76 But rumour has been set going so strongly that they boldly burst
   into speech.
      81 And make them go and hang themselves.

Stint, brodels, your din—yea, everyone!   *cease; scoundrels*
I rede that ye harken to I be gone;   *advise; till*
For if I begin, I break every bone,
85   And pull from the skin the carcass anon,
Yea, pardie!   *by God*
Cease all this wonder,
And make us no blunder;   *trouble*
For I rive you asunder,
90   Be ye so hardy.

Peace, both young and old, at my bidding, I rede,
For I have all in wold: in me stands life and dead.
Who that is so bold, I brain him through the head;
Speak not ere I have told what I will in this stead.   *place*
95   Ye wot not
All that I will move;   *do*
Stir not but ye have leave,   *unless*
For if ye do, I cleave
You small as flesh to pot.   *for the*

100   My mirths are turned to teen, my meekness into ire,   *grief*
And all for one, I ween, within I fare as fire.
May I see him with een, I shall give him his hire;   *eyes; due*
But I do as I mean, I were a full lewd sire
In wones.
105   Had I that lad in hand,
As I am king in land,
I should with this steel brand
Break all his bones.

My name springs far and near: the doughtiest, men
      me call,
110   That ever ran with spear, a lord and king royal.
What joy is me to hear a lad to seize my stall!
If I this crown may bear, that boy shall buy for all.   *pay*

92 For I have all at my command: I have power of life and death.
93 Whoever is bold enough [to speak].
101 i.e. I burn within.
103–4 Unless I do as I intend, I shall be considered a foolish fellow everywhere.
111 What joy it is for me to hear of a lad who will seize my throne!

I anger: *grow angry*
I wot not what devil me ails.
115   They teen me so with tales
That, by God's dear nails,
I will peace no longer.

What devil! methinks I burst for anger and for teen;
I trow these kings be past, that here with me have
    been.
120   They promised me full fast ere now here to be   *firmly*
    seen,
For else I should have cast another sleight, I ween.
I tell you,
A boy they said they sought
With offering that they brought;
125   It moves my heart right nought
To break his neck in two.

But be they passed me by, by Mahoun in heaven,
I shall, and that in hie, set all on six and seven.   *in haste*
Trow ye a king as I will suffer them to neven   *appoint*
130   Any to have mastery but myself full even?   *indeed*
Nay, lieve!—   *believe me*
The devil me hang and draw,
If I that losel know,
But I give him a blow
135   That life I shall him reave.

For perils yet I would wist if they were gone;
And ye thereof hear told, I pray you say anon;   *if*
For and they be so bold, by God that sits in throne,
The pain cannot be told that they shall have
    ilkone,   *everyone*
140   For ire.
Such pains heard never man tell,

114–17 I don't know what the devil is wrong with me. They annoy
me so with [seditious] talk that, by God's dear nails (i.e. the nails of the
cross), I will keep silent no longer.
121 I would have planned another ruse, I think.
132–6 Once I know who the scoundrel is, may the devil hang and draw
me if I don't give him a blow that will kill him. Yet because of the dangers
[that threaten me] I would like to know if they are gone.

For-ugly and for-fell,
That Lucifer in hell
Their bones shall all to-tear.   *tear apart*

145 *I Soldier.*   Lord, think not ill if I tell you how they
          are past;
     I keep not lain, truly.   Since they came by you last,
     Another way in hie they sought, and that full fast.
     Herod.   Why, and are they past me by?   We! out!
          for teen I burst!
     We! fie!

150   Fie on the devil!   Where may I bide,
      But fight for teen and all to-chide?
      Thieves, I say ye should have spied,   *scoundrels*
      And told when they went by.

      Ye are knights to trust!   Nay, losels ye are, and
          thieves!
155   I wot I yield my ghost, so sore my heart it grieves.
     2 Sold.   What need you be abashed?   There are no
          great mischiefs
      For these matters to gnast.
     3 Sold.   Why put ye such repriefs   *reproofs*
      Without cause?
      Thus should ye not threat us,
160   Ungainly to beat us;   *improperly*
      Ye should not rehete us   *rebuke*
      Without other saws.

     Herod.   Fie, losels and liars!   Lurdans ilkone!   *rascals*
      Traitors and well worse!   Knaves, but knights none!
165   Had ye been worth your ears, thus had they not
          gone;
      Get I those land-leapers, I break ilka bone.   *vagabonds*

142 Most horrible and cruel.
146 I don't wish to hide anything, truly.
148 Alas, alack!   I am bursting with rage.
150–1 Where can I stay without fighting and brawling with rage?
155–7 I know I shall give up the ghost, for my heart grieves so sorely. . . .
Why should you be upset?   The harm done is not so great that you
need gnash your teeth about it.
162 i.e. without our saying anything in our own defence.

First vengeance
Shall I see on their bones;
If ye bide in these wones,   *this place*
170 I shall ding you with stones—   *hit*
Yea, ditizance doutance.   *without doubt*

I wot not where I may sit for anger and for teen;
We have not done all yet, if it be as I ween.
Fie! devil! now how is it?   As long as I have een,
175 I think not for to flit, but king I will be seen   *flee*
For ever.
But stand I to quart,
I tell you my heart:
I shall gar them start,   *make*
180 Or else trust me never.

    1 Sold.   Sir, they went suddenly ere any man wist;   *knew*
Else had met we—yea, pardie!—and may ye trust.
    2 Sold.   So bold nor so hardy against our list
Was none of that company durst meet me with fist
185 For feard.   *fear*
    3 Sold.   Ill durst they abide,   *scarcely*
But ran them to hide;   *themselves*
Might I them have spied,
I had made them a beard.

190 What could we more do to save your honour?
    1 Sold.   We were ready thereto, and shall be ilk   *every*
        hour.
    Herod.   Now since it is so, ye shall have favour,
Go where ye will go, by town and by tower.
Go hence!
195 I have matters to mell   *discuss*
With my privy counsel.   [*The Soldiers retire.*
Clerks, ye bear the bell;   [*To the Counsellors.*
Ye must me insense.   *inform*

177–8 But if I stay in good health, I tell you what I intend.
183–4 There was none of that company so boldly defiant of us that he
dared fight me.
189 I would have outwitted them.
197 i.e. you are the best.

One spake in mine ear a wonderful talking,
200 And said a maiden should bear another to be king.
Sirs, I pray you inquire in all writing,
In Virgil, in Homer, and all other thing
But legend.
Seek poesy tales,   *tales in verse*
205 Leave epistles and grales.   *graduals*
Mass, matins, nought avails—
All these I defend.   *forbid*

I pray you tell hendly now what ye find.   *promptly*
  1 Counsellor.   Truly, sir, prophecy, it is not blind.
210 We read thus by Isay: He shall be   *in Isaiah*
    so kind   *conceived*
That a maiden, soothly, which never sinned,
Shall him bear:
Virgo concipiet,
Natumque pariet.
215 'Emmanuel' is het,   *is he called*
His name for to lere:

'God is with us,' that is for to say.
  2 Couns.   And others say thus, trust me ye may:
Of Bedlem a gracious lord shall spray,   *spring*
220 That of Jewry mightious king shall be ay,
Lord mighty;
And him shall honour
Both king and emperor.
  Herod.   Why, and should I to him cower?
225 Nay, there thou liest lightly!   *readily*

Fie! the devil thee speed, and me, but I drink once! *unless*
This hast thou done, indeed, to anger me for the
    nonce;

203 i.e. a passage from Scripture or the lives of saints.
213-14 A virgin shall conceive, and bear a son.
216 To inform you of his name.
227 On purpose to anger me.

And thou, knave, thou thy meed shall have, by
    Cock's dear bones!
Thou canst not half thy creed!   Out, thieves,
    from my wones!
230 Fie, knaves!
Fie, dottypolls, with your books: *blockheads*
Go cast them in the brooks!
With such wiles and crooks   *tricks*
My wit away raves.

235 Heard I never such a trant, that a knave so slight
Should come like a saint and reave me my right.
Nay, he shall aslant; I shall kill him down straight.
Ware! I say, let me pant.   Now think I to fight   *breathe*
For anger.
240 My guts will out-thring   *burst out*
But I this lad hang;
Without I have avenging
I may live no longer.

Should a carl in a cave but of one year of age   *churl*
245 Thus make me to rave?
  1 Couns.   Sir, peace this outrage!
Away let ye waive all such language.
Your worship to save, is he aught but a page
Of a year?
We two shall him teen
250 With our wits between,
That, if ye do as I mean,   *say*
He shall die on a spear.

---

228 *Cock's*, a corrupt form of 'God's.'
229 You don't know half your creed, i.e. you don't know your ABC.
234 I'm going out of my mind.
235 I never heard of such a trick, that a fellow so worthless.
237 He shall come to grief; I shall kill him off straight away.
244 A reference to the cave in which Christ was born, according to the apocryphal gospel known as the Protevangelium.
245–50 Sir, suppress this fury! Have done with all such language. Saving your reverence, is he anything but a boy of a year old? We two (i.e. the two Counsellors) shall harm him with the help of our combined wits.

  2 Couns. For dread that he reign, do as we rede:
   Throughout Bedlem and ilk other stead
255 Make knights ordain, and put unto dead
   All knave-children of two years' breed
   And within;
   This child may ye spill   *destroy*
   Thus at your own will.
260 *Herod.* Now thou say'st heretill   *about this*
   A right noble gin.   *stratagem*

   If I live in land good life, as I hope,
   This dare I thee warrant—to make thee a pope.
   Oh, my heart is risand now in a glope!
265 For this noble tidand thou shalt have a drop *news*
   Of my good grace:
   Marks, rents, and pounds,   *revenues*
   Great castles and grounds;
   Through all seas and sounds
270 I give thee the chase.

   Now will I proceed and take vengeance. [*To Messenger:*
   All the flower of knighthead call to legeance, *allegiance*
   Beausire, I thee bid; it may thee advance. *fair sir*
  Mess. Lord, I shall me speed and bring, perchance,
275 To thy sight. [*He goes to summon the Soldiers.*
   Hark, knights, I you bring
   Here new tiding:
   Unto Herod king
   Haste with all your might,

280 In all haste that ye may, in armour full bright;
   In your best array look that ye be dight.   *clad*
  1 Sold. Why should we fray?   *fight*
  2 Sold.   This is not all right.
  3 Sold. Sirs, without delay I dread that we fight.
  Mess. I pray you,

  255–7 Make knights prepare, and put to death all male children of two
years old and under.
  264 My heart is rising now and beating wildly.
  269–70 I give you the right of hunting everywhere.

285   As fast as ye may
      Come to him this day.
    1 Sold. What, in our best array?
    Mess. Yea, sirs, I say you.

    2 Sold. Somewhat is in hand, whatever it mean.
290 *3 Sold.* Tarry not for to stand, there ere we have
        been.   *[They go to Herod.*
    Mess. King Herod all-wieldand, well be ye seen!
      Your knights are coming in armour full sheen,   *bright*
      At your will.
    1 Sold. Hail, doughtiest of all!
295   We are come at your call
      For to do what we shall,   *must*
      Your lust to fulfil.   *wishes*

    Herod. Welcome, lordings, iwis, both great and   *indeed*
        small!
    The cause now is this that I send for you all:
300   A lad, a knave, born is, that should be king royal;
    But I kill him and his, I wot I burst my gall.
    Therefore, sirs,
    Vengeance shall ye take
    All for that lad's sake,
305   And men I shall you make,
    Where ye come aywhere, sirs.

    To Bedlem look ye go, and all the coast about;   *region*
    All knave-children ye slay—and lords ye shall be
      stout—   *valiant*
    Of years if they be two and within. Of all that rout, *crowd*
310   Alive leave none of tho that lie in swaddle-clout,
    I rede you.
    Spare no kins blood,   *kind of*
    Let all run on flood;
    If women wax wood,   *mad*
315   I warn you, sirs, to speed you.   *hurry*

    290–1 Don't stand loitering about before we have been there (i.e. to see
Herod). . . . Almighty King Herod, may you be well!
    305–6 And I shall make you men of importance, wherever you go, sirs.
    310 Leave alive none of those who lie in swaddling-clothes.

      Hence!   Now go your way, that ye were there.

  2 Sold.   I wot we make a fray, but I will go before.   *attack*

  3 Sold.   Ah! think, sirs, I say; I mun whet like a boar.

  1 Sold.   Set me before, ay good enough for a score.

320   Hail, hendly!   *gracious (king)*

      We shall for your sake

      Make a doleful lake.   *sport*

  Herod.   Now if ye me well wrake,   *avenge*

      Ye shall find me friendly.

[Scene II.   *Another part of Bethlehem*]

325 *2 Sold.*   Go we now to our note and handle them well.

  3 Sold.   I shall pay them on the coat, begin I to reel.

  1 Sold.   Hark, fellows!   Ye dote.   Yonder comes
      unsele;

      I hold here a groat she likes me not well   *bet*

      By we part.   *by the time*

330   Dame, think it not ill,

      Thy knave if I kill.   *boy*

  1 Woman.   What, thief, against my will?

      Lord, keep him in quart!   *safe*

  1 Sold.   Abide now, abide; no farther thou goes.

335 *1 Wom.*   Peace, thief! Shall I chide and make here a
      noise?

  1 Sold.   I shall reave thee thy pride; kill we these boys!

  1 Wom.   Tide may betide, keep well thy nose,

      False thief!

      Have on loft on thy hood!

---

316 So that you may get there quickly.

318–19 I must whet my tusks like a boar. . . .   Put me in front, for I 'm
as good as a score of knights at any time.

325–7 Let us now go about our business and handle them (i.e. the
children) well. . . .   I shall give them a thrashing if I really let myself
go. . . .   You talk foolishly.   Yonder comes misfortune (i.e. someone who
is going to be unlucky).

336 I shall rob you of your pride and joy.

337 Come what may, guard your nose well.

339 Here's a blow aimed high at your hood!

340 *1 Sold.* What, whore, art thou wood?   *mad*
    1 Wom. Out, alas, my child's blood!
    Out, for reprief!   *shame*

    Alas for shame and sin!   Alas that I was born!
    Of weeping who may blin, to see her child forlorn? *cease*
345 My comfort and my kin, my son thus all
        to-torn!   *torn to pieces*
    Vengeance for this sin I cry, both even and morn.
    2 Sold. Well done!
    Come hither, thou old stry: *hag*
    That lad of thine shall die.
350 *2 Wom.* Mercy, lord, I cry!
    It is mine own dear son.

    2 Sold. No mercy thou move; it mends thee not,
        Maud.
    2 Wom. Then thy scalp shall I cleave!   List thou
        be clawed?
    Leave, leave, now beleave!
    2 Sold.   Peace, bid I, bawd!
355 *2 Wom.* Fie, fie, for reprief!   Fie, full of fraud—
    No man!
    Have at thy tabard,
    Harlot and holard: *rascal; fornicator*
    Thou shalt not be spared!
360 I cry and I ban!   *curse*

    Out! murder-man, I say, strong traitor and   *murderer*
        thief!
    Out, alas, and welaway! my child that was me lief! *dear*
    My love, my blood, my play, that never did man   *joy*
        grief!
    Alas, alas, this day!   I would my heart should cleave
365 Asunder!
    Vengeance I cry and call

    352 You 'll move no mercy; it will not help you, Maud.
    353–4 Do you want to be clawed?   Leave off!
    355–6 Imposter—no true man!

On Herod and his knights all:
Vengeance, Lord, upon them fall,
And mickle world's wonder!

370 *3 Sold.*   This is well-wrought gear that ever may be.
Come hitherward here!   Ye need not to flee.
3 Wom.   Will ye do any dere to my child and me?   *harm*
3 Sold.   He shall die, I thee swear; his heart's
blood shalt thou see.
3 Wom.   God forbid!
375 Thief, thou shedest my child's blood!
Out, I cry!   I go near wood!
Alas, my heart is all on flood,
To see my child thus bleed.

By God, thou shalt abuy this deed that thou hast   *pay for*
done.
380 *3 Sold.*   I rede thee not, stry, by sun and by moon!
3 Wom.   Have at thee, say I!   Take thee there a foin!   *jab*
Out on thee, I cry!   Have at thy groin   *snout*
Another!
This keep I in store.
385 *3 Sold.*   Peace now, no more!
3 Wom.   I cry and I roar,
Out on thee, man's murderer!

Alas, my babe, mine innocent, my fleshly get!   For
sorrow
That God me dearly sent, of bales who may me
borrow?
390 Thy body is all to-rent!   I cry, both even and   *torn*
morrow,
Vengeance for thy blood thus spent: 'Out!' I cry,
and 'Harrow!'

369–70 And great earthly grief! ...   This is a job well done.
380 No, I tell you, hag.
384 I'll keep this one in reserve.
388–9 The offspring of my flesh!   Because of the sorrow that God has
so dearly sent me, who can save me from misery?
391 'Help, help!' I cry.

1 Sold.   Go lightly!   *quickly*
 Get out of these wones,
 Ye trots, all at once,   *hags*
395 Or by Cock's dear bones
 I make you go wightly!   *swiftly*

 They are flayed now, I wot; they will not abide. *frightened*
 2 Sold.   Let us run foot-hot—now would I we   *hot-foot*
  hied—
 And tell of this lot, how we have betide.
400 *3 Sold.*   Thou canst do thy note; that have I espied.   *work*
 Go forth now,
 Tell thou Herod our tale.
 For all our avail,   *help*
 I tell you, sans fail   *without*
405 He will us allow.   *praise*

 1 Sold.   I am best of you all, and ever have been;
 The devil have my soul but I be first seen!
 It sits me to call 'my lord', as I ween.
 2 Sold.   What needs thee to brawl?   Be not so keen
410 In this anger.
 I shall say thou didst best—
 Save myself, as I gest.   [*Aside.*   *thought*
 1 Sold.   We! that is most honest.
 3 Sold.   Go, tarry no longer.

[SCENE III.   *Herod's palace*]

415 *1 Sold.*   Hail Herod, our king!   Full glad may
  ye be;
 Good tidings we bring.   Harken now to me:
 We have made riding throughout Jewry.   *a mounted raid*
 Well wit ye one thing, that murdered have we
 Many thousands.

 399 And tell of our lot, how we have fared.
 408 It is fitting to call me 'my lord', I think.
 418 Be assured of one thing.

420 *2 Sold.*   I held them full hot,
        I paid them on the coat;
        Their dames, I wot,
        Never bind them in bands.

    3 Sold.   Had ye seen how I fared when I came
              among them!
425   There was none that I spared, but laid on and
              dang them.   *beat*
        I am worthy a reward.   Where I was among them,
        I stood and I stared; no pity to hang them
        Had I.
    Herod.   Now by mighty Mahoun,
430   That is good of renown,   *of good fame*
        If I bear this crown
        Ye shall have a lady

    Ilkone to him laid, and wed at his will.
    1 Sold.   So have ye long said—do somewhat theretill!
435 *2 Sold.*   And I was never flayed for good nor for ill.
    3 Sold.   Ye might hold you well paid our lust to fulfil,
        Thus think me,
        With treasure untold,
        If it like that ye would
440   Both silver and gold
        To give us great plenty.

    Herod.   As I am king crowned, I think it good right;   *quite*
        There goes none on ground that has such a   *earth*
            wight.   *person* (*to serve him*)
        A hundred thousand pound is good wage for a
            knight;
445   Of pence good and round, now may ye go light
        With store;
        And ye knights of ours

420–3 I made it hot for them, I gave them a thrashing; their mothers,
I know, will never again wrap them in swaddling-clothes.
    434–8 Do something about it! . . . And I was never scared for any
reason. . . .   You might consider yourself well pleased, it seems to me,
to satisfy our desire with untold treasure.
    445–6 Now you can go quickly with plenty of money.

Shall have castles and towers,
Both to you and to yours,
450 For now and evermore.

  1 Sold. Was never none born by downs ne by dales,
         Nor yet us beforn, that had such   *before our time*
           avails.   *benefits*
  2 Sold. We have castles and corn, much gold in   *bags*
           our mails.
  3 Sold. It will never be worn, without any tales.
455   Hail, hendly!
         Hail, lord! Hail, king!
         We are forth founding.   *going*
  Herod.   Now Mahoun he you bring
         Where he is lord friendly.

[*The Soldiers retire. Herod addresses the audience:*

460 Now in peace may I stand—I thank thee, Mahoun!—
     And give of my land that longs to my crown.   *belongs*
     Draw, therefore, nearhand, both of burgh and of   *near*
       town:
     Marks, ilkone, a thousand, when I am boun,
     Shall ye have;
465 I shall be full fain
     To give that I sayn.   *say*
     Wait when I come again,
     And then may ye crave.

     I set by no good, now my heart is at ease,
470 That I shed so mickle blood. Peace, all my
       riches!   *kingdoms*
     For to see this flood from the foot to the nose
     Moves nothing my mood; I laugh that I   *so much that*
       wheeze.
     Ah, Mahoun,
     So light is my soul,

454 It (i.e. the gold) will never be used up, truly.
458–9 Now may Mahomet bring you to where he is friendly lord (i.e.
to hell).
469 I set no store by it.

475   That all of sugar is my gall!
    I may do what I shall,
    And bear up my crown.

    I was casten in care, so frightly afraid;   *fearfully*
    But I thar not despair, for low is he laid   *need*
480   That I most dreaded ere, so have I him flayed;   *defeated*
    And else wonder were—and so many strayed
    In the street—
    That one should be harmless
    And scape away hafless,
485   Where so many childs
    Their bales cannot beet.

    A hundred thousand, I wot, and forty are slain,
    And four thousand.   Thereat me ought to be fain;
    Such a murder on a flat shall never be again.   (*level*) *place*
490   Had I had but one bat at that lurdan   *blow*
    So young,
    It should have been spoken
    How I had me wroken,
    Were I dead and rotten,
495   With many a tongue.

    Thus shall I teach knaves example to take,
    In their wits that raves, such mastery to make.
    All wantonness waives; no language ye crack!
    No sovereign you saves; your necks shall I shake
500   Asunder.
    No king ye on call
    But on Herod the royal,
    Or else many one shall
    Upon your bodies wonder.   *marvel at*

476–9 I can do what I must, and maintain my crown.
483–6 That one should be unharmed and escape away, helpless as he was, when so many children cannot mend their injuries (i.e. cannot come to life again).
488 I ought to be glad about it.
492–5 After I was dead and rotten, many a tongue would have told how I avenged myself.
497–8 Who are mad enough to claim such power. Put away all arrogance; don't speak boastfully!
501 Petition no king.

505   For if I hear it spoken when I come again,
Your brains be broken; therefore be ye bain.   *obedient*
Nothing be unlocken; it shall be so plain.
Begin I to rocken, I think all disdain
For-daunch.
510   Sirs, this is my counsel:
Be not too cruel.
But adieu!—to the devil!
I can no more French.   *know*

505   If I hear any more rebellious talk.
507 Nothing shall be explained, i.e. no explanations will be needed or given.
508–9 If I begin to behave violently, I shall think all indignation too squeamish (i.e. I shan't spare anyone's feelings).

THE WOMAN TAKEN IN ADULTERY

There are counterparts in the York and Chester cycles of this N. town pageant, which is based on John viii. 3–11. But the N. town playwright shows greater skill both in dramatizing the scene of the adultery and in heightening the excitement of the battle of wits between Christ and the Pharisees. The action is vividly presented and the dialogue rings true: it would be difficult to find a more successful example of a biblical story grafted on to the stem of medieval life. But while the human interest of the episode is exploited to the full, its Christian meaning—the quality of divine mercy—is also made plain.

The Banns of the N. town cycle whet the interest of the spectators by describing the horns of the dilemma prepared for Christ by the Pharisees:

> They conceived this subtlety:
> If Christ this woman did damn truly,
> Against his preaching then did he,
> Which was of pity and of mercy;
> And if he did her save,
> Then were he against Moses' law,
> That biddeth with stones she should be slaw [slain];
> Thus they thought under their awe [power]
> Christ Jesu for to have.

The pageant amplifies the brief biblical verses in such a way as to bring out the nature of Christ's dilemma and the device by which He turns the tables on His enemies. It is written in octaves rhyming *ababbcbc*.

CHARACTERS

JESUS

SCRIBE   YOUNG MAN

PHARISEE   WOMAN

ACCUSER

THE WOMAN TAKEN IN ADULTERY

[SCENE I.   *The Temple*]

Jesus.   Nolo mortem peccatoris.

	Man, for thy sin take repentance;	*make*
	If thou amend that is amiss,	*that which*
	Then heaven shall be thine inheritance.	
5	Though thou have done against God grievance,	*offence*
	Yet mercy to ask look thou be bold;	
	His mercy doth pass, in true balance,	
	All cruel judgment by manifold.	*many times over*

	Though that your sins be never so great,	
10	For them be sad and ask mercy;	
	Soon of my Father grace ye may get,	
	With the least tear weeping out of your eye.	
	My Father me sent thee, man, to buy:	*redeem*
	All thy ransom myself must pay,	
15	For love of thee myself will die;	
	If thou ask mercy, I say never nay.	

	Unto the earth from heaven above,	
	Thy sorrow to cease and joy to restore,	*end*
	Man, I came down all for thy love;	
20	Love me again, I ask no more.	*in return*
	Though thou mishap and sin full sore,	*come to grief*
	Yet turn again and mercy crave.	
	It is thy fault and thou be lore;	*if; lost*
	Ask thou mercy and thou shalt have.	

25	Upon thy neighbour be not vengeable,	*vengeful*
	Against the law if he offend.	
	Like as he is, thou art unstable;	
	Thine own frailty ever thou attend.	*see to*

1 I do not want the sinner to die.
6 Yet see that you have the courage to ask for mercy.
7 Doth exceed, [if weighed] in a true balance.

133

Evermore thy neighbour help to amend,
30   Even as thou wouldest he should thee;
Against him wrath if thou accend,   *kindle*
The same in hap will fall on thee.   *perhaps*

Each man to other be merciable,   *merciful*
And mercy he shall have at need;
35   What man of mercy is not treatable,
When he asketh mercy he shall not speed.   *prosper*
Mercy to grant I come indeed:
Whoso ask mercy he shall have grace;   *whoever*
Let no man doubt for his misdeed,   *fear*
40   But ever ask mercy while he hath space.   *time*

[SCENE II.   *Another part of the Temple*]

Scribe.   Alas, alas, our law is lorn!   *ruined*
A false hypocrite, Jesu by name,
That of a shepherd's daughter was born,
Will break our law and make it lame.
45   He will us work right mickle shame,
His false purpose if he uphold;   *carries out*
All our laws he doth defame—
That stinking beggar is wondrous bold!

Pharisee.   Sir scribe, in faith that hypocrite
50   Will turn this land all to his lore;   *teaching*
Therefore I counsel him to indict,
And chastise him right well therefor.
Scr.   On him believe many a score,
In his preaching he is so gay: *excellent*
55   Each man him followeth more and more;
Against that he saith no man saith nay.

Phar.   A false quarrel if we could feign,
That hypocrite to put in blame,
All his preaching should soon distain,   *be disgraced*
60   And then his worship should turn to shame.   *honour*

35 Whatever man is not inclined to mercy.
45 He will do us very great shame.

With some falsehood to spill his name,
Let us essay his lore to spill;
The people with him if we could grame,   *make angry*
Then should we soon have all our will.

65 *Accuser*.   Hark, sir Pharisee, and sir scribe!
A right good sport I can you tell;
I undertake that right a good bribe
We all shall have to keep counsel.   *keep it secret*
A fair young quean hereby doth dwell,
70 Both fresh and gay upon to look,
And a tall man with her doth mell: *handsome; meddle*
The way unto her chamber right even he took.   *straight*

Let us three now go straight thither:
The way full even I shall you lead;
75 And we shall take them both together,
While that they do that sinful deed.
Scr.   Art thou siker that we shall speed?
Shall we him find when we come there?
Acc.   By my troth, I have no dread
80 The hare from the form we shall arear.

Phar.   We shall have game, and this be true.   *if*
Let us three work by one assent:
We will her bring even before Jesu,
And of her life the truth present,
85 How in adultery her life is lent.   *spent*
Then him before when she is brought,
We shall him ask the true judgment,
What lawful death to her is wrought.

61–2 By ruining his reputation with some falsehood, let us try to undo his teaching.
65 *Accuser*, a man who accused or prosecuted in a court of justice.
74 I shall show you the way indeed.
77 Are you sure we shall be successful?
79–80 Upon my word, I have no doubt we shall start the hare from its form.
82 Act in unison.
88 Is laid down for her.

Of grace and mercy ever he doth preach,
90   And that no man should be vengeable.
Against the woman if he say wreak,
Then of his preaching he is unstable;
And if we find him variable   *changeable*
Of his preaching that he hath taught,   *in*
95   Then have we cause, both just and able,
For a false man that he be caught.   *arrested*

Scr.   Now, by great God, ye say full well!
If we find him in variance,
We have good reason, as ye do tell,
100 Him for to bring to foul mischance.
If he hold still his dalliance,
And preach of mercy, her for to save,
Then have we matter of great substance
Him for to kill and put in grave.

105 Great reason why I shall you tell:
For Moses doth bid in our law
That every adulterer we should quell,   *kill*
And yet with stones they should be slaw.   *slain*
Against Moses' law if that he draw,   *go*
110 That sinful woman with grace to help,   *mercy*
He shall never escape out of our awe,   *power*
But he shall die like a dog whelp.   *puppy*

Acc.   Ye tarry over-long, sirs, I say you;
They will soon part, as that I guess;
115 Therefore if ye will have your prey now,
Let us go take them in their wantonness.
Phar.   Go thou before, the way to dress;   *guide*
We shall thee follow within short while.
If that we may that quean distress,
120 I hope we shall Jesu beguile.

91 If he says the woman should be punished.
101 If he keeps up his idle talk.
103 Substantial cause.

[SCENE III.   *Outside the woman's house*]

Scr.   Break up the door and go we in;
    Set to the shoulder with all thy might.
    We shall take them even in their sin;
    Their own trespass shall them indict.

    Here a young man runs out in his doublet, with shoes
      untied and holding up his breeches with his hand,
      and Accuser says :

125 *Acc.*   Stow that harlot, some earthly wight,
    That in adultery here is found.
    Young Man.   If any man stow me this night,
    I shall him give a deadly wound.

    If any man my way doth stop,
130   Ere we depart dead shall he be: *part*
    I shall this dagger put in his crop;   *gullet*
    I shall him kill ere he shall me.
    Phar.   Great God's curse mote go with thee!   *may*
    With such a shrew will I not mell.   *villain*
135 *Young Man.*   That same blessing I give you three,
    And bequeath you all to the devil of hell.

    In faith, I was so sore afraid   [*To audience.*
    Of yon three shrews, the sooth to say,
    My breech be not yet well uptied;
140   I had such haste to run away.
    They shall never catch me in such a fray;
    I am full glad that I am gone.
    Adieu, adieu, a twenty devil way!
    And God's curse have ye every one.

122 Put your shoulder to it with all your strength.
125 Somebody arrest that villain.
143 The devil take you.

145 *Scr.*   Come forth, thou stot; come forth, thou scout!
　　　Come forth, thou bismer and brothel bold!
　　　Come forth, thou whore and stinking
　　　　bitch-clout!　　　　　　　　　　　*lewd baggage*
　　　How long hast thou such harlotry hold?　　*kept up*
　　Phar.   Come forth, thou quean; come forth, thou
　　　　scold!
150　　Come forth, thou sloven; come forth, thou slut!
　　　We shall thee teach with cares cold
　　　A little better to keep thy cut.

　　Woman.   Ah, mercy, mercy, sirs, I you pray;
　　　For God's love have mercy on me!
155　　Of my misliving me not bewray:
　　　Have mercy on me, for charity!　　*in the name of charity*
　　Acc.   Ask us no mercy; it shall not be.
　　　We shall so ordain for thy lot
　　　That thou shalt die for thine adultery;
160　　Therefore come forth, thou stinking stot!

　　Wom.   Sirs, my worship if ye will save,　　　*honour*
　　　And help I have no open shame,
　　　Both gold and silver ye shall have,
　　　So that in cleanness ye keep my name.
165 *Scr.*   Meed for to take, we were to blame,
　　　To save such stots; it shall not be.
　　　We shall bring thee to such a game
　　　That all adulterers shall learn by thee.

　　Wom.   Standing ye will not grant me grace,　　*since*
170　　But for my sin that I shall die,
　　　I pray you kill me here in this place,
　　　And let not the people upon me cry.

145 *stot*, heifer (as a word of abuse); *scout*, a term of contempt.
146 You lewd creature and bold harlot.
151–2 We shall teach you with bitter grief to behave yourself a little better.
155 Do not expose me for my evil living.
165–6 We should be to blame if we accepted a bribe for saving such wantons.
167 We shall make such game of you.

If I be slandered openly,
To all my friends it shall be shame;
175 I pray you kill me privily:
Let not the people know my defame.   *infamy*

Phar. Fie on thee, scout! The devil thee quell!
Against the law shall we thee kill?
First shall hang thee the devil of hell,
180 Ere we such follies should fulfil.   *commit*
Though it like thee never so ill,
Before the prophet thou shalt have law:
Like as Moses doth charge us till,
With great stones thou shalt be slaw.

185 *Acc.* Come forth apace, thou stinking scout!   *quickly*
Before the prophet thou were this day,   *defend yourself*
Or I shall give thee such a clout
That thou shalt fall down even in the way.   *street*
Scr. Now, by great God, and I thee pay,
190 Such a buffet I shall thee take   *give*
That all the teeth, I dare well say,
Within thy head forthy shall shake.   *because of it*
        [*They take her to Jesus.*

[SCENE IV. *The Temple*]

Phar. Hark, sir prophet! We all you pray
To give true doom and just sentence   *judgment*
195 Upon this woman, which this same day
In sinful adultery hath done offence.

*Here Jesus, while they are accusing the woman, shall
all the time write on the ground with his finger.*

Acc. See, we have brought her to your presence
Because ye be a wise prophet,
That ye shall tell by conscience
200 What death to her ye think most meet.

181 However much you dislike the idea.
182 *prophet*, a mocking reference to Christ.
183 Just as Moses charges us to do.
189 If I pay you [what is due to you].
199 So that you shall tell truly.

Scr.   In Moses' law right thus we find:
 That such false lovers shall be slain;
 Straight to a stake we shall them bind,   *straightway*
 And with great stones burst out their brain.
205 Of your conscience tell us the plain,   *plain fact*
 With this woman what shall be wrought: *done*
 Shall we let her go quit again,   *free*
 Or to her death shall she be brought?

Jesus does not reply, but goes on writing on the ground.

Wom.   Now, holy prophet, be merciable!   *merciful*
210 Upon me, wretch, take no vengeance.
 For my sins abominable,
 In heart I have great repentance.
 I am well worthy to have mischance,
 Both bodily death and worldly shame;
215 But, gracious prophet, of succurrance
 This time pray you, for God's name.

Phar.   Against the law thou didst offence,
 Therefore of grace speak thou no more;
 As Moses giveth in law sentence,
220 Thou shalt be stoned to death therefor.
Acc.   Have done, sir prophet, tell us your lore: *advice*
 Shall we this woman with stones kill,
 Or to her house, her home, restore?
 In this matter tell us your will.

225 *Scr.*   In a cold study methinketh ye sit;   *brown*
 Good sir, awake, tell us your thought:
 Shall she be stoned?—tell us your wit—   *opinion*
 Or in what rule shall she be brought?
Jesus.   Look which of you that never sin wrought, *committed*
230 But is of life cleaner than she;
 Cast at her stones, and spare her nought,
 Clean out of sin if that ye be.

215–16 This time, in God's name, [I] pray you for help.
228 Or what disciplinary action shall be taken against her?
232 If you are entirely free from sin.

*Here Jesus, again stooping down, shall write on the
    ground, and all the accusers, as if put to shame,
    shall go apart into three separate places.*

    Phar.   Alas, alas, I am ashamed!
       I am afeard that I shall die;   *afraid*
235   All my sins, even properly named,
       Yon prophet did write before mine eye.
       If that my fellows that did espy,
       They will tell it both far and wide;
       My sinful living if they out cry,
240   I wot never where my head to hide.

    Acc.   Alas, for sorrow mine heart doth bleed!
       All my sins yon man did write;
       If that my fellows to them took heed,
       I cannot me from death acquit.
245   I would I were hid somewhere out of sight,
       That men should me nowhere see ne know;   *nor*
       If I be take, I am afflight
       In mickle shame I shall be throw.

    Scr.   Alas the time that this betid!   *happened*
250   Right bitter care doth me embrace;   *grief*
       All my sins be now unhid: *revealed*
       Yon man before me them all doth trace.
       If I were once out of this place,
       To suffer death great and vengeance able,
255   I will never come before his face,
       Though I should die in a stable.

    Wom.   Though I be worthy for my trespass
       To suffer death abominable,
       Yet, holy prophet, of your high grace,
260   In your judgment be merciable.
       I will never more be so unstable:
       O holy prophet, grant me mercy!
       Of my sins unreasonable   *for*
       With all my heart I am sorry.

   247–8 If I am caught, I am afraid I shall be put to great shame.
   254 Liable [as I am] to suffer death and vengeance.

265 *Jesus.*   Where be thy foemen that did thee accuse?
     Why have they left us two alone?
    Wom.   Because they could not themselves excuse,
     With shame they fled hence every one.
     But, gracious prophet, list to my moan:
270   Of my sorrow take compassion;
     Now all mine enemies hence be gone,
     Say me some word of consolation.

    Jesus.   For those sins that thou hast wrought
     Hath any man condemned thee?
275 *Wom.*   Nay, forsooth, that hath there nought;
     But in your grace I put me.
    Jesus.   For me thou shalt not condemned be;
     Go home again and walk at large:
     Look that thou live in honesty,
280   And will no more to sin, I thee charge.

    Wom.   I thank you highly, holy prophet,
     Of this great grace ye have me grant;   *granted*
     All my lewd life I shall down let,   *forsake*
     And fond to be God's true servant.   *try*
285 *Jesus.*   What man of sin be repentant,   *whatever*
     Of God if he will mercy crave,
     God of mercy is so abundant,
     That what man ask it he shall it have.

     When man is contrite and hath won grace,
290   God will not keep old wrath in mind;
     But better love to them he has,
     Very contrite when he them find.
     Now God, that died for all mankind,
     Save all these people both night and day;
295   And of our sins he us unbind,
     High Lord of heaven that best may.   Amen.

269 Listen to my lament.
275 No, truly, no one has done that.
287 God is so abounding in mercy.
294–6 Bring all these people to salvation both night and day (i.e.
always); and may He deliver us from our sins, the high Lord of heaven
who is best able to do so.

The York Pageant of the Pinners
and Painters

THE CRUCIFIXION

The liturgical playwrights seem to have made little use of the Passion theme, perhaps because the central rite of the Mass was felt to be an incomparable enactment of Christ's self-sacrifice. But the Passion plays, including the Crucifixion, had a large share in all the Corpus Christi cycles, and the deep impression that they made is still traceable in a stanza of the traditional carol *The Seven Virgins*:

> Go you down, go you down to yonder town,
> And sit in the gallery;
> And there you'll find sweet Jesus Christ,
> Nailed to a big yew-tree.
> (*Oxford Book of Carols*, p. 91.)

The Crucifixion is dramatized with restraint in the Chester and N. town cycles, but the York and Towneley pageants on this subject make a direct assault on the feelings of the audience. The York pageant is attributed to an unknown playwright of extraordinary talent who, for want of a better name, is usually called the 'York realist.' His flair for realistic presentation of the physically horrible is nowhere more in evidence than in this pageant, where the business of the Crucifixion is mercilessly drawn out 'until this performance of a heavy manual job by a set of rough workmen becomes a Bosch-like nightmare' (McNeir, p. 622).

One horrible detail—the pulling at cords to stretch out Christ's limbs as far as the nail-holes—may have originated with the medieval playwrights, who had in any case to use cords to attach to the Cross the player acting the part of Christ Crucified. What may be a very close representation of the staging of the Crucifixion can be seen in some of the English alabaster carvings (see Hildburgh, plate xvii. d).

The Pinners, or pinmakers, who joined with the painters in producing this pageant, presumably made a grimly competent job of handling the 'hammers and nails large and long' used by the executioners.

The pageant is written in a twelve-line stanza rhyming *abababababcdcd*, with four stresses in *a, b* and three in *c, d*.

CHARACTERS

JESUS   FOUR SOLDIERS

THE CRUCIFIXION

[SCENE. *Calvary*]

1 Soldier.   Sir knights, take heed hither in hie:
This deed undree we may not draw;
Ye wot yourselves as well as I
How lords and leaders of our law
5   Have given doom that this dote shall die.   *fool*
2 Sold.   Sir, all their counsel well we know.
Since we are come to Calvary,
Let ilk man help now as him owe.   *each; ought*
3 Sold.   We are all ready, lo,
10   That forward to fulfil.   *agreement*
4 Sold.   Let hear how we shall do,
And go we tite theretill.   *quickly to it*

1 Sold.   It may not help here for to hone,   *delay*
If we shall any worship win.
15 *2 Sold.*   He must be dead needlings by noon.   *of necessity*
3 Sold.   Then it is good time that we begin.
4 Sold.   Let ding him down!   Then is he done.   *knock*
He shall not dere us with his din.   *harm*
1 Sold.   He shall be set and learned soon,
20   With care to him and all his kin.   *sorrow*
2 Sold.   The foulest death of all
Shall he die for his deeds.
3 Sold.   That means cross him we shall.
4 Sold.   Behold, so right he redes.

25 *1 Sold.*   Then to this work us must take heed,
So that our working be not wrong.
2 Sold.   None other note to neven is need,
But let us haste him for to hang.

1–2 Quickly pay attention to me: we cannot do this deed negligently.
19 He shall be beaten and soon taught a lesson.
23–4 That means we shall crucify him. . . .   See, he advises rightly.
27 There is no need to mention any other sort of work (i.e. other than hanging).

    3 Sold.   And I have gone for gear, good speed,   *quickly*
30   Both hammers and nails large and long.
    4 Sold.   Then may we boldly do this deed;
    Come on, let kill this traitor strong.
    1 Sold.   Fair might ye fall in fere,
    That have wrought on this wise.   *in this way*
35 *2 Sold.*   Us needs not for to lere   *we need; learn*
    Such faitours to chastise.   *impostors*

    3 Sold.   Since ilka thing is right arrayed,   *every; arranged*
    The wiselier now work may we.
    4 Sold.   The cross on ground is goodly graid,   *made ready*
40   And bored even as it ought to be.   *bored with holes*
    1 Sold.   Look that the lad on length be laid,
    And made be ta'en unto this tree.
    2 Sold.   For all his fare he shall be flayed: *boasting; terrified*
    That on essay soon shall ye see.
45 *3 Sold.*   Come forth, thou cursed knave,
    Thy comfort soon shall keel.   *grow cold*
    4 Sold.   Thine hire here shalt thou have.   *payment*
    1 Sold.   Walk on! Now work we well.

    Jesus.   Almighty God, my Father free,   *noble*
50   Let these matters be marked in mind:
    Thou bade that I should buxom be,   *ready*
    For Adam's plight to be pined.   *tortured*
    Here to death I oblige me,   *pledge myself*
    From that sin for to save mankind,
55   And sovereignly beseech I thee   *above all*
    That they for me may favour find;
    And from the fiend them fend,   *defend*
    So that their souls be safe
    In wealth withouten end;   *happiness*
60   I keep not else to crave.

33 Good luck to you all.
41-2 See that the fellow is laid lengthwise and fastened to this cross.
44 That you shall soon see when we try.
60 I have no wish to ask for anything else.

1 Sold. We! hark, sir knights, for Mahound's blood!
  Of Adam's kind is all his thought.   *race*
2 Sold. The warlock waxes worse than wood;
  This doleful death ne dreadeth he nought. *painful*
65 *3 Sold.* Thou shouldst have mind, with main and
    mood,
  Of wicked works that thou hast wrought.
4 Sold. I hope that he had been as good
  Have ceased of saws that he up sought.
1 Sold. Those saws shall rue him sore,
70 For all his sauntering, soon.
2 Sold. Ill speed them that him spare *bad luck to*
  Till he to death be done!

3 Sold. Have done belive, boy, and make thee boun,
  And bend thy back unto this tree. [*Jesus lies down.*
75 *4 Sold.* Behold, himself has laid him down,
  In length and breadth as he should be.
1 Sold. This traitor here tainted of treason, *convicted*
  Go fast and fetter him then, ye three;
  And since he claimeth kingdom with crown,
80 Even as a king here hang shall he.
2 Sold. Now, certes, I shall not fine *certainly; stop*
  Ere his right hand be fast.
3 Sold. The left hand then is mine;
  Let see who bears him best.

85 *4 Sold.* His limbs on length then shall I lead,
  And even unto the bore them bring. *hole*
1 Sold. Unto his head I shall take heed,
  And with my hand help him to hang.
2 Sold. Now since we four shall do this deed,
90 And meddle with this unthrifty thing, *unprofitable*

61 *We!*, an exclamation of surprise; *for . . . blood*, by Mahomet's blood.
 63 The sorcerer waxes worse than mad, i.e. behaves worse than a
madman.
 65 You should try hard to remember.
 67–70 I think he would have done well to stop telling those tales he
made up. . . . Soon he shall bitterly regret all his babbling.
 73 Be quick, knave, and get ready.
 84 Let's see who acquits himself best.
 85 Then I shall draw his limbs to their full length.

Let no man spare for special speed,
Till that we have made ending.

3 Sold.   This forward may not fail;
Now we are right arrayed.   *properly prepared*

95 *4 Sold.*   This boy here in our bail   *knave; charge*
Shall bide full bitter braid.

1 Sold.   Sir knights, say now, work we ought?

2 Sold.   Yes, certes, I hope I hold this hand.   *think*

3 Sold.   And to the bore I have it brought
100   Full buxomly withouten band.

1 Sold.   Strike on then hard, for him thee bought.

2 Sold.   Yes, here is a stub will stiffly stand;
Through bones and sinews it shall be sought.
This work is well, I will warrant.

105 *1 Sold.*   Say, sir, how do we there?
This bargain may not blin.

3 Sold.   It fails a foot and more;
The sinews are so gone in.

4 Sold.   I hope that mark amiss be bored.

110 *2 Sold.*   Then must he bide in bitter bale.   *grievous torment*

3 Sold.   In faith, it was over-scantily scored;
That makes it foully for to fail.   *badly*

1 Sold.   Why carp ye so?   Fast on a cord,   *prate; fasten*
And tug him to, by top and tail.

115 *3 Sold.*   Yea, thou commandest lightly as a lord;   *readily*
Come help to hale him, with ill hail!

91 Let no one use less than his best possible speed.
93 i.e. we must not fail to carry out our agreement.
96 Shall suffer a most bitter onslaught.
97 Are we doing anything? (The First Soldier is evidently in charge.)
100 Quite obediently without [having to use a] rope.
101 By Him who redeemed you.
102–3 Here is a nail that will stand fast; [in order to find it] we shall
have to look for it through bones and sinews.
106–8 This business may not cease, i.e. must go on. . . . It (the hole)
is out by a foot or more; his sinews are so shrunken.
109 I think that mark is bored wrongly, i.e. the hole has not been bored
in the place marked for it.
111–12 i.e. the mark was put in the wrong place; that 's why the hole
is badly out.
114 And tug him to [the holes] by his head and feet.
116 Come and help to pull him, confound you!

1 Sold.   Now certes that shall I do—
Full snelly as a snail.   *quickly*
3 Sold.   And I shall tache him to,
120   Full nimbly with a nail.

This work will hold, that dare I heet,   *promise*
For now are fest fast both his hend.
4 Sold.   Go we all four then to his feet,
So shall our space be speedily spent.
125   *2 Sold.*   Let see what bourd his bale might beet;
Thereto my back now would I bend.
4 Sold.   Oh! this work is all unmeet: *unfit*
This boring must all be amend.   *improved*
1 Sold.   Ah, peace, man, for Mahoun!
130   Let no man wot that wonder;
A rope shall rug him down,   *pull*
If all his sinews go asunder.

2 Sold.   That cord full kindly can I knit,   *properly*
The comfort of this carl to keel.   *churl*
135   *1 Sold.*   Fest on then fast that all be fit;
It is no force how fell he feel.
2 Sold.   Lug on, ye both, a little yet.
3 Sold.   I shall not cease, as I have sele.
4 Sold.   And I shall fond him for to hit.   *try*
140   *2 Sold.*   Oh, hale!   *pull*
4 Sold.   Ho now!   I hold it well.
1 Sold.   Have done, drive in that nail,
So that no fault be found.
4 Sold.   This working would not fail,
If four bulls here were bound.

118 A sarcastic aside by the First Soldier, who considers himself a
foreman, not a workman.
119 Fasten him to [the cross].
122 For now both his hands are firmly fastened.
124–5 So shall our time be well spent. . . . Let's see what jest can
lighten his misery.
130 Let no one know about this extraordinary thing. (The First
Soldier seems to believe that their work has been undone by magic.)
135–6 Get hold of it firmly then so that all shall be ready; it doesn't
matter how cruelly he feels it.
138 As I hope for happiness.

145 *1 Sold.*   These cords have evil increased his pains,   *severely*
       Ere he were till the borings brought.   *bore-holes*
  2 Sold.   Yea, asunder are both sinews and veins
       On ilka side, so have we sought.
  3 Sold.   Now all his gauds nothing him gains;   *tricks*
150   His sauntering shall with bale be bought.
  4 Sold.   I will go say to our sovereigns
       Of all these works how we have wrought.
  1 Sold.   Nay, sirs, another thing
       Falls first to you and me:
155   They bade we should him hang
       On high that men might see.

  2 Sold.   We wot well so their words were;
       But, sir, that deed will do us dere.   *harm*
  1 Sold.   It may not mend for to moot more;
160   This harlot must be hanged here.   *rascal*
  2 Sold.   The mortice is made fit therefor.   *ready for it*
  3 Sold.   Fest on your fingers then, in fere.
  4 Sold.   I ween it will never come there;   *think*
       We four raise it not right to-year.
165 *1 Sold.*   Say, man, why carp'st thou so?
       Thy lifting was but light.   *feeble*
  2 Sold.   He means there must be mo   *more*
       To heave him up on height.   *high*

  3 Sold.   Now certes, I hope it shall not need
170   To call to us more company.
       Methink we four should do this deed,
       And bear him to yon hill on high.
  1 Sold.   It must be done, without dread.   *doubt*
       No more, but look ye be ready,
175   And this part shall I lift and lead;   *carry*
       On length he shall no longer lie.   *prone*

148 Everywhere, so far as we have looked.
150 His babbling shall be paid for with suffering.
152 How well we have done our work.
157 We know well that their words were so, i.e. that they said so.
159 It won't help to argue any more.
162 Fasten your fingers on to it then, all together.
164 We four won't lift it upright this year.
174 No more [talking].
175 *this part*, i.e. the head of the cross.

Therefore now make ye boun:
Let bear him to yon hill.
4 *Sold.*   Then will I bear here down,
180   And tent his toes until.

2 *Sold.*   We two shall see till either side,
For else this work will wry all wrong.   *go*
3 *Sold.*   We are ready, good sirs.   Abide,
And let me first his feet up fong.   *take*
185 2 *Sold.*   Why tent ye so to tales this tide?
1 Sold.   Lift up!   [*They lift the cross.*
4 *Sold.*   Let see!
2 *Sold.*   Oh, lift along!   .   *lengthwise*
3 *Sold.*   From all this harm he should him hide,   *protect*
And he were God.   *if*
4 *Sold.*   The devil him hang!
1 Sold.   For-great harm have I hent: *very great; suffered*
190   My shoulder is asunder.
2 *Sold.*   And certes I am near shent,   *exhausted*
So long have I borne under.   *held it up*

3 *Sold.*   This cross and I in two must twin,   *part*
Else breaks my back asunder soon.
195 4 *Sold.*   Lay down again and leave your din;
This deed for us will never be done.
                                    [*They lay it down.*
1 Sold.   Essay, sirs, let see if any gin   *contrivance*
May help him up withouten hone;   *delay*
For here should wight men worship win,   *valiant*
200   And not with gauds all day to gone.
2 *Sold.*   More wighter men than we
Full few I hope ye find.
3 *Sold.*   This bargain will not be,
For certes me wants wind.

179–80 Then I will carry him down here (i.e. at the foot of the cross),
and attend to his toes.
181 i.e. to each arm of the cross.
185 Why do you now listen to such talk [when there's work to be done]?
200 And not spend all day playing pranks.
203–4 This business won't get finished, for certainly I am short of
breath.

205 4 *Sold.*   So will of work never we were;
I hope this carl some cautels cast.
2 *Sold.*   My burden sat me wondrous sore;   *grieved*
Unto the hill I might not last.
1 *Sold.*   Lift up, and soon he shall be there;
210 Therefore fest on your fingers fast.
3 *Sold.*   Oh, lift!   [*They lift up the cross again.*
1 *Sold.*   We lo!   *ah well*
4 *Sold.*   A little more.
2 *Sold.*   Hold then!
1 *Sold.*   How now!
2 *Sold.*   The worst is past.
3 *Sold.*   He weighs a wicked weight.
2 *Sold.*   So may we all four say,
215 Ere he was heaved on height,
And raised in this array.   *fashion*

4 *Sold.*   He made us stand as any stones,
So boistous was he for to bear.
1 *Sold.*   Now raise him nimbly for the nonce,
220 And set him by this mortice here;
And let him fall in all at once,
For certes that pain shall have no peer.
3 *Sold.*   Heave up!
4 *Sold.*   Let down, so all his bones
Are asunder now on sides sere.
            [*They drop the cross into its mortice.*
225 1 *Sold.*   This falling was more fell   *painful*
Than all the harms he had;
Now may a man well tell   *count*
The least lith of this lad.   *limb; fellow*

3 *Sold.*   Methinketh this cross will not abide,   *stand firm*
230 Ne stand still in this mortice yet.   *nor*

205–6 We were never at such a loss in our work; I think this fellow has
played some tricks [of magic].
217–18 He brought us to a standstill; he was so bulky to carry.
219 *for the nonce*, a metrical tag.
223–4 So that all his bones break asunder everywhere.

4 *Sold.*   At the first time was it made over-wide:
    That makes it wave, thou mayst well wit.   *move; know*
1 *Sold.*   It shall be set on ilka side,
    So that it shall no further flit;   *move*
235 Good wedges shall we take this tide,
    And fest the foot, then all is fit.
2 *Sold.*   Here are wedges arrayed   *prepared*
    For that, both great and small.
3 *Sold.*   Where are our hammers laid,
240 That we should work withal?   *with*

4 *Sold.*   We have them here even at our hand.
2 *Sold.*   Give me this wedge; I shall it in drive.
4 *Sold.*   Here is another yet ordand.
3 *Sold.*   Do take it me hither belive.
245 1 *Sold.*   Lay on then fast.
3 *Sold.*   Yes, I warrant
    I thring them sam, so mote I thrive.
    Now will this cross full stably stand;   *firmly*
    All if he rave, they will not rive.
1 *Sold.* [*to Christ*]   Say, sir, how likes you now   *do you like*
250 This work that we have wrought?
4 *Sold.*   We pray you say us how
    Ye feel, or faint ye aught.

Jesus.   All men that walk by way or street,
    Take tent ye shall no travail tine;
255 Behold my head, my hands, my feet,
    And fully feel now, ere ye fine,   *stop*
    If any mourning may be meet,   *fitting*
    Or mischief measured unto mine.   *misfortune*

231 *it*, i.e. the mortice.
232 *it*, i.e. the cross.
233 Fixed on each side.
243-4 Here is yet another made ready. . . . Bring it here to me quickly.
246 I shall press them (i.e. wedge and cross) together, as I hope to
prosper.
248 Even if he raves, they will not tear apart.
252 Or whether you are faint at all.
254 Take care that you waste none of my suffering.

My Father, that all bales may beet,
260   Forgive these men that do me pine.
What they work wot they nought;
Therefore, my Father, I crave,
Let never their sins be sought,   *examined*
But see their souls to save.

265 *1 Sold.*   We! hark! he jangles like a jay.   *chatters*
    2 Sold.   Methink he patters like a pie.   *magpie*
    3 Sold.   He has been doing so all day,
    And made great moving of mercy.
    4 Sold.   Is this the same that gan us say   *did*
270   That he was God's Son almighty?
    1 Sold.   Therefore he feels full fell affray,
    And deemed this day for to die.   *was judged*
    2 Sold.   *Vah! qui destruis templum. . .*
    3 Sold.   His saws were so, certain.   *words*
275 *4 Sold.*   And, sirs, he said to some
    He might raise it again.

    1 Sold.   To muster that he had no might,   *show*
    For all the cautels that he could cast;   *tricks; play*
    All if he were in word so wight,
280   For all his force now he is fast.
    As Pilate deemed, is done and dight;
    Therefore I rede that we go rest.
    2 Sold.   This race mun be rehearsed right,
    Through the world both east and west.
285 *3 Sold.*   Yea, let him hang there still,
    And make mows on the moon.   *grimaces at*
    4 Sold.   Then may we wend at will.   *go*
    1 Sold.   Nay, good sirs, not so soon.

259 Who may remedy all ills.
260–1 That inflict suffering on me.   They know not what they do.
264 But see that their souls are saved.
268 i.e. made a great show of moving God to mercy.
271 That is why he suffers this deadly assault.
273 Ah, thou that destroyest the temple (Mark xiv. 58, John ii. 19).
279 Even if he was so valiant in word.
281 It is done and performed as Pilate decreed.
283 This action must be rightly reported.

For certes us needs another note:
290 This kirtle would I of you crave.
　　2 *Sold.* Nay, nay, sir, we will look by lot
　　Which of us four falls it to have.
　　3 *Sold.* I rede we draw cut for this coat—   *advise; lots*
　　Lo, see how soon—all sides to save.
295 4 *Sold.* The short cut shall win, that well ye wot,
　　Whether it fall to knight or knave.
　　1 Sold. Fellows, ye thar not flite,   *need; wrangle*
　　For this mantle is mine.
　　2 *Sold.* Go we then hence tite;   *quickly*
300 This travail here we tine.

289 For, to be sure, there's another thing we need to do.
291–2 We shall draw lots to see which of us four is to have it.
294 To protect all our interests.
300 We are wasting our efforts here.

THE HARROWING OF HELL

This episode of Christ's descent into hell has its main source in the apocryphal gospel of Nicodemus, chaps. xviii ff. (see M. R. James). A popular medieval legend, it is dramatized in all the English cycles, represented in sculpture and painted glass, and used again and again in the sermons. In non-dramatic literature it makes its most impressive appearance in *Piers Plowman*, which comes to a grand climax in the vision of the Harrowing of Hell (B-text, Passus xviii). The ubiquity of this legend in the Middle Ages is an illustration of the fact that 'the preaching, the art, the drama, and the literature were all bent to the same end of instruction in the supposed facts of Christian history and of moral exhortation, revealing the immense weight of theological sway and proclaiming themselves as sides of a dominant core of ideas' (E. M. W. Tillyard, *The English Epic and Its Background*, London, 1954, p. 150).

In the pageant as we now have it the descent into hell is followed by a descent into a seamy corner of medieval life. The final scene of the offending ale-wife, funny though it is, has nothing whatever to do with the rest of the pageant and may well be a later addition.

The Cooks and Innkeepers of Chester who acted this pageant no doubt enjoyed themselves, rushing in and out of the monstrous jaws of hell-mouth and clashing their pots and kettles. But it should be remembered that medieval men and women took the devil and his works more seriously than we do to-day, and that the merriment of the spectators probably had an uncomfortable edge to it.

CHARACTERS

JESUS	ARCHANGEL MICHAEL
ADAM	DAVID
ISAIAH	ENOCH
SIMEON	ELIAS
JOHN THE BAPTIST	THE SAVED THIEF
SETH	A WOMAN

THREE DEMONS, *including* SATAN

THE HARROWING OF HELL

[Scene I.   *Hell*]

[A great light begins to shine]

Adam. Ah, Lord and sovereign Saviour,
Our comfort and our counsellor,
Of this light thou art author,
As I see well in sight.

5 This is a sign thou wouldst succour
Thy folk that be in great languor,   *distress*
And of the devil be conqueror,
As thou hast yore behight.   *promised long ago*

Me thou madest, Lord, of clay,
10 And gave me Paradise in to play;
But after my sin, sooth to say,
Deprived I was therefro,   *thereof*
And from that weal put away;
And here have lenged sithen ay
15 In thesterness, both night and day,   *darkness*
And all my kind also.

Now, by this light that I now see,
Joy is comen, Lord, through thee;   *come*
And of thy people thou hast pity,
20 To put them out of pain.
Siker it may none other be,   *surely*
But now thou hast mercy on me;
And my kind, through thy postie,
Thou wilt restore again.

4 As I plainly see with my own eyes.
14 And here have remained ever since.
23-4 And, through thy power, thou wilt restore my race (i.e. mankind)
to a state of grace.

159

25 *Isaiah.*   Yea, sikerly, this ilk light   *surely; same*
          Comes from God's Son almight,   *almighty*
          For so I prophesied aright,
          While that I was living.
          Then I to all men behight,   *promised*
30   As I ghostly saw in sight,   *spiritually*
          This word that I through God's might
          Shall rehearse without tarrying: *repeat*

          The people, that time I said express,   *plainly*
          That went about in thesterness,
35   See a full great lightness,   *would see*
          As we do now, each one.
          Now is fulfilled my prophecy,
          That I, the prophet Isay,
          Wrote in my books that will not lie,
40   Whoso will look thereon.

     Simeon.   And I, Simeon, sooth to say,
          Will honour God, all that I may;
          For when Christ a child was, in good fay,   *truly*
          In temple I him took;
45   And as the Holy Ghost that day
          Taught me, ere I went away,
          These words I said to God's pay,   *at God's pleasure*
          As men may find in Book: *Bible*

          There I prayed, without lease,   *lie*
50   That God would let me die in peace;
          For he is Christ that comen was,
          I had both felt and seen,
          That he had ordained for man's heal,
          Joy to the people of Israel.
55   Now is it wonnen, that ilk weal,
          To us, withouten ween.

          33–5 Isa. lx. 3.
          49–50 Luke ii. 29.
          51–6 For I had both felt and seen that he who had come was Christ,
     whom God had ordained for man's salvation and to give joy to the people
     of Israel.   Now is that happiness won for us, without doubt.

John.   Yea, Lord, I am that ilk John
         That followed thee in flood Jordan,   *river*
         And that in world about can gone   *did go*
60   To warn of thy coming.
         And with my finger I showed express
         A meek lamb in thy likeness,
         In token that thou comen was
         Mankind of bale to bring.   *from woe*

65 *Seth.*   And I, Seth, Adam's son, am here,
         That living went, withouten were,   *doubt*
         To ask at Paradise a prayer   *favour*
         At God, as I shall say: *of*
         That he would grant an angel in hie   *quickly*
70   To give oil of his mercy,
         To anoint my father in his nye,   *suffering*
         In sickness when he lay.

         Then to me appeared Michael,
         And bade me travail never a deal,
75   And said weeping nor prayers fele   *many*
         Availed me nothing to seek.
         Nay, of that oil might I have none,
         Made I never so much moan,
         Until five thousand years were gone,
80   And five hundred eke.   *also*

                   They all kneel.

David.   Ah, high God and King of bliss,
         Worshipped be thy name, iwis!   *indeed*
         I hope that time now comen is
         To deliver us of danger.
85   Come, Lord!   Come to hell anon,
         And take out thy folk, every one,
         For those years are fully gone
         Since mankind first came here.

61-4 John i. 29.
74 And told me not to trouble myself at all.
76 Did not avail me at all in my quest.

Then let Satan, sitting on his throne, say to the demons :

  Satan. Hell hounds, all that be here,
90 Make you boun with boast and bere, *ready ; clamour*
  For to this fellowship in fere   *together*
  There hies a ferly freke.   *fearsome man*
  A noble morsel you have mun: *shall have*
  Jesu, that is God's Son,
95 Comes hither with us to won;   *dwell*
  On him now ye you wreak!   *avenge yourselves*

  A man is he fully, in fay,
  For greatly death he dreaded to die,
  And these words I heard him say:
100 'My soul is thirsty unto death.'   *eager for*
  Such as I made halt and blind,
  He hath healed into their kind;
  Therefore that boaster look that you bind
  In bale of hell breath.   *torment ; reek*

105 *2 Demon.* Sir Satanas, what man is he
  That should thee prive of thy postie? *deprive ; power*
  How dare he do against thee,   *act*
  And dread his death to die?
  Greater than thou he seems to be;
110 For degraded of thy degree   *from*
  Thou must be soon, well I see,
  And prived of thy prey.

  3 Dem. Who is this, so stiff and strong, *stalwart*
  That masterly comes us among,
115 Our fellowship that he would fong?   *capture*
  But thereof he shall fail.
  Wite he us with any wrong,   *reproach*
  He shall sing a sorry song;
  But on thee, Satanas, it is long,
120 And his will aught avail.

97 He is, in truth, nothing but a man.
100 Matt. xxvi. 38.
102 He has restored them to their natural state.
119-20 But, Satan, it is due to you if his will avails at all.

 Sat. Against this shrew that comes here   *rascal*
   I tempted the folk in foul manner;
   Aisel and gall to his dinner   *vinegar; for*
   I made them for to dight,   *prepare*
125 And hang him on a rood-tree.
   Now he is dead right so through me;
   And to hell, as you shall see,
   He comes anon in hight.   *haste*

 2 Dem. Satan, is not this that sire
130 That raised Lazar out of the fire?
 Sat. Yea, this is he that will conspire
   Anon to reave us all.   *rob*
 3 Dem. Out, out! Alas, alas!
   Here I conjure thee, Satanas,
135 Thou suffer him not come to this place,
   For aught that may befall.

 2 Dem. Yea, sikerly, and he come here, *if*
   Passed is clean our power;
   For all this fellowship in fere   *together*
140 He may take away when he would,
   For all be at his commandment:
   Lazar, that was with us lent,   *dwelling*
   Maugre our teeth away he went,
   And him might we not hold.

  Then shall come Jesus, and a clamour shall be made, or
  a loud sound of things striking together, and let
  Jesus say: 'Lift up your heads, O ye gates; and be
  ye lift up, ye everlasting doors; and the King of glory
  shall come in.'

145 *Jesus.* Open hell gates anon,
   You princes of pain, every one,
   That God's Son may in gone,   *go in*
   And the King of bliss!

  130 *fire*, i.e. hell fire.
  143 In spite of our teeth, i.e. in spite of all we could do.

    2 Dem. Go hence, poplard, from this place,   *hypocrite*
150   Or thou shalt have a sorry grace!
    For all thy boast and thy menace,
    These men thou shalt miss.   *fail to get*

    Sat. Out, alas! What is this?
    Saw I never so much bliss
155   Toward hell come, iwis,
    Since I was prince here.
    My masterdom now fares amiss,   *dominion*
    For yonder a stubborn fellow is,
    Right as wholly hell were his,   *as if*
160   To reave me of my power.

    3 Dem. Yea, Satanas, thy sovereignty
    Fails clean; therefore flee,
    For no longer in this see   *throne*
    Here shalt thou not sit.
165   Go forth! Fight for thy degree,   *rank*
    Or else our prince shalt thou not be;
    For now passeth thy postie,
    And hence thou must flit.   *depart*

        Then let them hurl Satan from his throne.

    Sat. Out, alas! I am shent;   *ruined*
170   My might fails, verament;   *truly*
    This prince that is now present
    Will spoil from me my prey.   *rob*
    Adam, by my enticement,
    And all his blood, through me were blent;   *deceived*
175   Now hence they shall all be hent,   *taken*
    And I in hell for ay.

    Jesus. Open up hell gates, yet I say,
    You princes of pine that be present,   *torment*
    And let the King of bliss this way,   *let pass*
180   That he may fulfil his intent.

                [He enters the gates of hell.

Sat.   Say, what is he, that King of bliss?
Jesus.   That Lord, the which almighty is.
There is no power like to his;
Of all joy he is king.
185   And to him is none like, iwis,
As is soothly seen by this,
For man, that sometime did amiss,
To his bliss he will bring.

Then Jesus shall take Adam by the hand.

Peace to thee, Adam, my darling,
190   And eke to all thine offspring
That righteous were in earth living;
From me you shall not sever.   *be parted*
To bliss now I will you bring;
There you shall be without ending.
195   Michael, lead these men singing
To joy that lasteth ever.

Michael.   Lord, your will done shall be.
Come forth, Adam, come with me!
My Lord upon the rood-tree
200   Your sins hath forbought.   *atoned for*
Now shall you have liking and lee,
And be restored to your degree,
That Satan with his subtlety
From bliss to bale hath brought.

Then Michael shall lead Adam and the saints to
Paradise; and in the way shall come Enoch and Elias
and the saved thief; and let Satan say:

205 *Sat.*   Out, alas!   Now goeth away
My prisoners and all my prey;
And I might not stir one stray,
I am so straitly dight.

201 Pleasure and protection.
207-8 And I cannot stir one straw (i.e. move an inch), I am so strictly
confined.

Now comes Christ, sorrow I may
210   For me and my meny for ay;   *company*
Never, since God made the first day,
Were we so foul of right.

[SCENE II.   *Paradise*]

Then Adam, seeing Enoch and Elias, says:

Adam.   Say, what manner of men be ye,
That bodily meet us, as I see,
215   And, dead, came not to hell as we,
Since all men damned were?
When I trespassed, God hight me   *promised*
That this place closed always should be
From earthly man to have entry;
220   And yet find I you here.

Enoch.   Sir, I am Enoch, sooth to say,
Put into this place to God's pay;   *at God's pleasure*
And here have lived ever since that day,
At liking all my fill.
225   And my fellow here, in good fay,   *faith*
Is Elias the prophet, as you see may,
That ravished was in that array,   *carried off; condition*
As it was God's will.

Elias.   Yea, bodily death, lieve thou me,   *believe*
230   Yet never suffered we;
But here ordained we are to be
Till Antichrist come with his.
Fight against us shall he,
And slay us in the holy city;
235   But, sikerly, within days three
And half one we shall rise.

212 Have we been so unfairly treated.
224 In pleasure to my heart's content.
232 *his,* i.e. his followers.

Adam.   And who is this that comes here
    With cross on shoulder in such manner?
Thief.   I am that thief, my father dear,
240   That hung on rood-tree;
    But for I lieved, withouten were,
    That Christ might save us both in fere,
    To him I made my prayer,
    The which was granted me.

245   When I saw signs veray   *sure*
    That he was God's Son, sooth to say,
    To him devoutly I can pray,   *did*
    In his realm when he come,
    To think on me by alway;   *always*
250   And he answered and said: 'This day
    In Paradise with me thou shalt be ay.'
    So hither the way I nome;

    And he betook me this tokening,   *granted*
    A cross upon my back hanging,
255   The angel Michael for to bring,
    That I might have entry.
Adam.   Go we to bliss, then, old and young,
    And worship God, alway wielding,   *ruling eternally*
    And afterward, I rede, we sing   *counsel*
260   With great solemnity:

    '*We praise thee, O God: we acknowledge thee to be*
    the Lord.'   And thus they shall go out glorifying
    God, singing 'Te Deum.'

[SCENE III.   *Hell*]

Woman.   Woe be to the time that I came here!
    I say to thee now, Lucifer,
    With all thy fellowship in fere,
    That present be in place: *here*

241 But because I believed, without doubt.
252 I made my way.

265   Woeful am I with thee to dwell,
    Sir Satanas, sergeant of hell;
    Endless pains and sorrow cruel
    I suffer in this place.

    Sometime I was a taverner,
270   A gentle gossip and a tapster,   *friend; barmaid*
    Of wine and ale a trusty brewer,
    Which woe hath me wrought.
    Of cans I kept no true measure:
    My cups I sold at my pleasure,
275   Deceiving many a creature,
    Though my ale were naught.   *bad*

    And when I was a brewer long,
    With hops I made my ale strong;
    Ashes and herbs I blent among,   *mixed in*
280   And marred so good malt.
    Therefore I may my hands wring,
    Shake my cans, and cups ring;
    Sorrowful may I sigh and sing,
    That ever I so dealt.

285   Taverners, tapsters of this city
    Shall be promoted here by me   *informed against*
    For breaking statutes of this country,
    Hurting the commonweal;
    With all tipplers, tapsters that are cunning,
290   Misspending much malt, brewing so thin,
    Selling small cups, money to win,
    Against all truth to deal.

    Therefore this place ordained is
    For such ill-doers, so much amiss.
295   Here shall they have their joy and bliss,
    Exalted by the neck,   *hung up*

274 I pleased myself about the amount of liquor I put in the cups I sold.
277 And when I had long been a brewer.
293–4 For such evil-doers, who have done so much wrong, this place is
therefore appointed.

With my master, mighty Mahoun,   *Mahomet*
For casting malt beside the comb,
Much water taking for to compound
300   And little of the sack.

With all masters, minglers of wine in the night,
Brewing so, blending against daylight;
Such new-made claret is cause full right
Of sickness and disease.
305   Thus I betake you, more and less,   *commend*
To my sweet master, sir Satanas,
To dwell with him in this place,
When it shall you please.

Sat.   Welcome, dear darling, to us all three;
310   Though Jesus be gone with our meny,
Yet shalt thou abide here still with me
In pain without end.

2 Dem.   Welcome, dear lady, I shall thee wed!
For many a heavy and drunken head,
315   Cause of thy ale, were brought to bed,   *because*
Far worse than any beast.
3 Dem.   Welcome, dear darling, to endless bale,
Using cards, dice, and cups small,
With many false oaths to sell thine ale;
320   Now thou shalt have a feast!

298–300 For putting malt anywhere but in the brewing-tub, taking a
lot of water to make the mixture and little from the sack (i.e. malt sack).
302 For diluting and blending their wine against the coming of day.

THE RESURRECTION

The York *Resurrection* is a late vernacular version of the oldest kind of Latin liturgical drama—the 'Easter Sepulchre' play, in which the three Marys at the empty tomb are shown receiving the news of the Resurrection from the angel. This liturgical play was itself a development of the Easter Mass trope, which is known as the *Quem quaeritis* from the two opening Latin words. A tenth-century example of the Easter trope from the monastery of St Gall (see Young, i. 201) may be translated as follows:

Angels. Whom do ye seek in the sepulchre, O Christian women?
Marys. Jesus of Nazareth who was crucified, O heavenly ones.
Angels. He is not here; He has risen even as He foretold. Go, announce that He has risen from the sepulchre.

A long and obscure history separates this simple dialogue from the York *Resurrection*. There are several early records of a liturgical *Resurrectio* acted in English churches on Easter Monday, although no texts have survived. There is also a reference, dating from the early thirteenth century, to a Resurrection play acted in the churchyard of Beverley Minster. This reference occurs in the well-known story of the boy who, while watching the play from the triforium of the Minster, fell to the ground and lay as if dead, but was miraculously restored to life by St John of Beverley.

The raw materials of the York *Resurrection* are largely drawn from liturgical drama, from the Bible and the apocryphal gospel of Nicodemus. Nevertheless, some of the best things in the pageant seem to owe nothing to literary sources, but to be due to the playwright's skill in setting the ancient story in the living context of his own age. Pilate, for example, is portrayed as a medieval magnate, steeped in every sort of subterfuge. When the soldiers report that the tomb is empty, it is Pilate who bribes them to spread the story that Christ's body has been carried off by armed force:

> Thus shall the sooth be bought and sold,
> And treason shall for truth be told.

The *Resurrection*, which is sometimes attributed to the 'York metrist' (see p. 1), is written in a six-line stanza rhyming *aaabab*. This stanza resembles the tail-rhyme of the Chester pageants, but has four instead of six *a*-verses. Concatenation, or stanza-linking by means of verbal repetition, is commonly used.

THE RESURRECTION

[Scene I. *The Judgment Hall*]

Pilate.   Lordings, listen now unto me,
I command you in ilk degree.
As doomsmen chief in this country,   *judges*
For counsel kenned,
5 At my bidding you owe to be   *ought*
And bainly bend.

And Sir Caiaphas, chief of clergy,
Of your counsel let hear in hie—
By your assent since we did die
10 Jesus this day—
If ye maintain, and stand thereby,
That work alway.

Caiaphas.   Yes, sir, that deed shall we maintain;
By law it was done all bedene,
15 Ye wot yourself, withouten ween,   *doubt*
As well as we.
His saws are now upon him seen,
And ay shall be.

Annas.   The people, sir, in this same stead,   *place*
20 Before you said with a wholehead
That he was worthy to be dead,

2 Each in his degree.
4 Known for your wise judgment.
6 And willingly obey.
8–12 Let us quickly hear your intention—since with your assent we have to-day put Jesus to death—whether you still uphold and stand by that deed.
14 It was all done legally.
17 His [evil] words are now visited upon him.
20 Unanimously affirmed in your presence.

173

And thereto swore;
Since all was ruled by righteous rede,   *counsel*
Neven it no more.   *mention*

25 *Pil.*   To neven methinketh it needful thing;
Since he was had to burying,   *taken*
Heard we neither of old ne young
Tidings between.
   Cai.   Centurion, sir, will bring tiding
30 Of all bedene.   *straightway*

We left him there for man most wise,   *as a man*
If any rebels would aught rise   *at all*
Our righteous doom for to despise   *judgment*
Or it offend,   *violate*
35 To seize them till the next assize
And then make end.

               [*Enter Centurion*]

Centurion.   Ah, blessed Lord, Adonai,
What may these marvels signify,
That here were showed so openly
40 Unto our sight
This day, when that the man gan die   *did*
That Jesus hight?   *was called*

It is a misty thing to mean;   *tell of*
So selcouth a sight was never seen,   *strange*
45 That to our princes and priests bedene,
Of this affray,
I will go wit withouten ween
What they can say.
               [*He approaches Pilate and the High Priests.*

27–8 We have heard no news of him from old or young (i.e. from anyone) in the interval.
   36 And then have their case tried and determined. (The reference is
to the medieval assize of Oyer and Terminer.)
   45–8 So that I will go straightway to our princes and priests and find
out for certain what they have to say about this alarming thing.

  God save you, sirs, on ilka side,   *everywhere*
50 Worship and wealth in worlds wide:
  With mickle mirth might ye abide,
  Both day and night.
  Pil. Centurion, welcome this tide,   *now*
  Our comely knight!

55 Ye have been missed us here among.
  Cent. God give you grace gradely to gang!
  Pil. Centurion, our friend full long,
  What is your will?
  Cent. I dread me that ye have done wrong
60 And wondrous ill.

  Cai. Wondrous ill? I pray thee, why?
  Declare it to this company.
  Cent. So shall I, sirs, tell you truly,
  Withouten train: *deceit*
65 The righteous man, then mean I by,
  That ye have slain.

  Pil. Centurion, cease of such saw!   *talk*
  Thou art a lered man in the law;   *learned*
  And if we should any witness draw   *cite*
70 Us to excuse,
  To maintain us evermore thee owe,
  And not refuse.

  Cent. To maintain truth is well worthy.   *very*
  I said you, when I saw him die,
75 That he was God's Son almighty
  That hangeth there;
  Yet say I so, and stand thereby
  For evermore.

  50 [And grant you] honour and prosperity the wide world over.
  55–6 You have been missed among us here. . . . God give you grace
 to prosper!
  65–6 I speak of the innocent man whom you have slain.
  71 You ought always to support us.

Cai.   Yea, sir, such reasons may ye rue;   *statements*
80   Ye should not neven such note anew,
        But ye could any tokenings true   *unless; signs*
        Unto us tell.
    Cent.   Such wonderful case never yet ye knew   *event*
        As now befell.

85 *Ann.*   We pray thee tell us of what thing.
    Cent.   All elements, both old and young,
        In their manners they made mourning
        In ilka stead,   *every*
        And knew by countenance that their king
90   Was done to death.

        The sun for woe he waxed all wan,   *dark*
        The moon and stars of shining blan;   *ceased*
        The earth trembled, and also man   *like*
        Began to speak;
95   The stones, that never were stirred ere then,
        Gan asunder break;

        And dead men rose, both great and small.
    Pil.   Centurion, beware withal!
        Ye wot our clerks eclipses call
100   Such sudden sight;
        Both sun and moon that season shall
        Lack of their light.

    Cai.   Yea, and if dead men rose bodily,
        That might be done through sorcery;
105   Therefore we set nothing thereby
        To be abashed.
    Cent.   All that I tell, for truth shall I
        Evermore trust.   *believe*

        80 You should not repeat such things.
        87 Each in its own way.
        89 And showed by their appearance.
        105–6 Therefore we do not consider it worth worrying about.

In this ilk work that ye did work,   *same*
110 Not alone the sun was murk;
But how your veil rove in your kirk,
That wit I would.
   Pil. Such tales full soon will make us irk,   *weary*
And they be told.   *if*

115 *Ann.* Centurion, such speech withdraw;
Of all these words we have no awe.
   Cent. Now since ye set nought by my saw,   *words*
Sirs, have good day!
God grant you grace that ye may know
120 The sooth alway.   *truth*

   Ann. Withdraw thee fast, since thou thee dreads,   *art afraid*
For we shall well maintain our deeds.
[Exit Centurion.
   Pil. Such wondrous reasons as he redes
Were never beforn.
125 *Cai.* To neven this note no more us needs,
Neither even ne morn.   *nor*

Therefore look no man make ill cheer;
All this doing may do no dere.   *harm*
But to beware yet of more were
130 That folk may feel,
We pray you, sirs, of these saws sere
Advise you well.

And to this tale take heed in hie,   *haste*
For Jesus said even openly
135 A thing that grieves all this Jewry,
And right so may—
That he should rise up bodily
Within the third day.

111–12 But I would like to know how the veil in your temple was rent.
123–5 Such wondrous events as he tells of were never before (i.e. never
happened before). . . . We need never mention this matter again.
127 Therefore see to it that none of you is downcast.
129–32 But in order to be on your guard against any further doubts that
folk may feel, we pray you, sirs, to consider carefully these various reports.
136 And rightly so.

And be it so, as mote I speed,
140 His latter deed is more to dread   *be feared*
Than is the first, if we take heed
Or tent thereto.   *notice*
To neven this note methink most need,
And best to do.

145 *Ann.*   Yea, sir, if all that he said so,
He has no might to rise and go,
But if his men steal him us fro
And bear away;
That were till us and other mo
150 A foul affray.

For then would they say, everilkone,   *every one*
That he rose by himself alone;
Therefore let him be kept anon   *guarded*
With knights hend,   *by; noble*
155 Unto three days be come and gone   *until*
And brought to end.

    Pil.   In certain, sirs, right well ye say,   *certainly*
For this ilk point now to purvey.   *arrange*
I shall ordain, if I may,   *contrive*
160 He shall not rise,
Nor none shall win him thence away   *take*
On no kins wise.

                 [*To his soldiers*:

Sir knights, that are in deeds doughty,
Chosen for chief of chivalry,   *flower*
165 As we ay in your force affy   *trust*
Both day and night,
Wend and keep Jesus' body
With all your might.

139 If it be so, as I hope to prosper.
143-4 I think it most needful to mention this matter, and best to do so.
145 Although he said so.
147 Unless his men steal him from us.
149-50 That would be a terrible fright for us and others as well.
162 By any means.

And for thing that ever be may,
170 Keep him well to the third day,   *till*
And let no man take him away
Out of that stead;
For, and they do, soothly I say   *if*
Ye shall be dead.

175 *I Soldier.*   Lordings, we say you for certain,
We shall keep him with might and main;
There shall no traitors with no train   *trickery*
Steal him us fro.
Sir knights, take gear that most may gain,   *avail*
180 And let us go.

[SCENE II.   *The Sepulchre*]

2 *Sold.*   Yes, certes, we are all ready boun;   *prepared*
We shall him keep till our renown.   *for the sake of*
On ilka side let us sit down
Now all in fere;   *together*
185 And soon we shall crack his crown,
Whoso comes here.   [*They fall asleep.*

Then an Angel sings 'Christ arising.'

[*Enter the three Marys*]

Magdalene.   Alas, to death I would be dight,   *put*
So woe in work was never wight!
My sorrow is all for that sight
190 That I gan see:
How Christ, my master most of might,
Is dead from me.

Alas, that I should see his pine,   *torment*
Or yet that I his life should tine!   *suffer the loss of*
195 Of ilka mischief he is medecine   *misfortune*
And bote of all,   *cure for*
Help and hold to ilka hine   *support; person*
That on him would call.

169 And whatever may befall.
188 No creature was ever so sad in all she does!
192 Is dead [and gone] from me.

Mary.   Alas, who shall my bales beet,
200   When I think on his wounds wet?
Jesus, that was of love so sweet,
And never did ill,
Is dead and graven under the greet   *buried; earth*
Withouten skill.   *reason*

205 *Salome.*   Withouten skill the Jews ilkone   *every one*
That lovely Lord have newly slain,
And trespass did he never none
In no kin stead.
To whom now shall I make my moan,
210   Since he is dead?

Magd.   Since he is dead, my sisters dear,
Wend we will on mild manner
With our anointments fair and clear,
That we have brought
215   To anoint his wounds on sides sere
That Jews him wrought.

Mary.   Go we sam, my sisters free;   *together; noble*
Full fair us longs his corpse to see,
But I wot not how best may be;
220   Help have we none,
And who shall now here of us three
Remove the stone?

Sal.   That do we not but we were mo,
For it is huge and heavy also.
225 *Magd.*   Sisters! A young child, as we go
Making mourning—
I see it sit where we wend to,
In white clothing.

199 Who shall assuage my sorrow.
208 Anywhere.
215 To anoint his various wounds.
218–19 We have a yearning desire to see his body, but I do not know
how it can best be done.
223 That we could not do unless there were more of us.
225 *A young child,* i.e. the Angel (Mark xvi. 5).

Mary.   Sisters, certes, it is not to hide:
230   The heavy stone is put beside.   *aside*
   Sal.   Certes, for thing that may betide   *anything*
      Near will we wend,
      To lait that lovely and with him bide   *seek*
      That was our friend.

[*An Angel speaks to them*]

235 *Angel.*   Ye mourning women in your thought,
      Here in this place whom have ye sought?
   Magd.   Jesus, that to death is brought,
      Our Lord so free.   *noble*
   Ang.   Women, certain here he is nought;
240   Come near and see.

      He is not here, the sooth to say;
      The place is void that he in lay.
      The sudary here see ye may,   *shroud*
      Was on him laid.   *which was*
245   He is risen and went his way,   *gone*
      As he you said.

      Even as he said, so done has he:
      He is risen through great postie;   *power*
      He shall be found in Galilee
250   In flesh and fell.
      To his disciples now wend ye
      And thus them tell.

   Magd.   My sisters dear, since it is so,
      That he is risen death thus fro,
255   As the Angel told me and you two—
      Our Lord so free—
      Hence will I never go
      Ere I him see.

229 Certainly, it is not to be hidden, i.e. is plain to see.
250 In flesh and skin, i.e. in the flesh.

Mary.　Mary, us thar no longer lend;
260　To Galilee now let us wend.
　　Magd.　Not till I see that faithful friend,
　　　My lord and leech;　　　　　　　　　　　　*healer*
　　　Therefore all this, my sisters hend,　　　　*gracious*
　　　That ye forth preach.

265　*Sal.*　As we have heard, so shall we say.
　　　Mary, our sister, have good day!
　　Magd.　Now very God, as he well may—　　　*true*
　　　Man most of might—
　　　He wis you, sisters, well in your way
270　And rule you right.　　　*[Exeunt Mary and Salome.*

　　　Alas, what shall now worth on me?
　　　My caitiff heart will break in three　　　　*miserable*
　　　When I think on that body free,
　　　How it was spilt:　　　　　　　　　　　　*destroyed*
275　Both feet and hands nailed till a tree,　　　*to*
　　　Withouten guilt.

　　　Withouten guilt the true was ta'en,
　　　For trespass did he never none:
　　　The wounds he suffered many one
280　Were for my miss;　　　　　　　　　　　　*wrongdoing*
　　　It was my deed he was for slain,
　　　And nothing his.

　　　How might I, but I loved that sweet—　　　*unless*
　　　That for my love tholed wounds wet,　　　*suffered*
285　And sithen be graven under the greet—　　　*afterwards*
　　　Such kindness kithe?　　　　　　　　　　*acknowledge*
　　　There is nothing to that we meet　　　　　*till*
　　　May make me blithe.

259　We need stay no longer.
264　Do you proclaim it.
269　May he guide you.
271　Alas, what will become of me now?
281-2　It was for my deeds he was slain, and not for his own.
285　And afterwards [allowed himself] to be buried in the earth.

[*She stands to one side.   The Soldiers awaken*]

1 Sold.   What! out, alas! what shall I say?
290   Where is the corpse that herein lay?
2 Sold.   What ails thee, man?   Is he away
    That we should tent?
1 Sold.   Rise up and see.
2 Sold.   Harrow! for ay
    I tell us shent.

295 *3 Sold.*   What devil is this?   What ails you two,
    Such noise and cry thus for to make too?   *to excess*
1 Sold.   Why is he gone?
3 Sold.   Alas, where is he that here lay?
4 Sold.   We! harrow! devil! where is he away?

300 *2 Sold.*   What! is he thusgates from us went,   *thus*
    That false traitor that here was lent,   *laid*
    And we truly here for to tent
    Had underta'en?
    Sikerly, I tell us shent   *certainly*
305   Wholly, ilkone.   *each of us*

3 Sold.   Alas, what shall we do this day,
    That thus this warlock is went his way?   *sorcerer*
    And safely, sirs, I dare well say
    He rose alone.
310 *2 Sold.*   Wit Sir Pilate of this affray,
    We mun be slain.

3 Sold.   Why, can none of us better rede?
4 Sold.   There is not else but we be dead.
2 Sold.   When that he stirred out of this stead

291–2 Has he, whom we had to watch over, gone away?
293–4 Help!   I think we are for ever ruined.
302–3 And whom we had undertaken to watch faithfully here.
310–13 If Pilate learns of this terrible thing we shall be slain. . . .
Why, does none of us know of a way out? . . .   We cannot escape being
put to death.

315   None could it ken.
   1 Sold.   Alas, hard hap was on my head   *luck*
    Among all men.

    Fro Sir Pilate wit of this deed,   *when; learns*
    That we were sleeping when he yede,   *went*
320   He will forfeit, withouten dread,   *confiscate; doubt*
    All that we have.
   2 Sold.   Us must make lies, for that is need   *necessary*
    Ourselves to save.

   3 Sold.   Yea, that rede I well, also mote I go.
325 *4 Sold.*   And I assent thereto also.
   2 Sold.   An hundred, shall I say, and mo,   *more*
    Armed ilkone,
    Came and took his corpse us fro,
    And us near slain.   *nearly slew*

330 *1 Sold.*   Nay, certes, I hold there none so good   *nothing*
    As say the sooth even as it stood,
    How that he rose with main and mood,   *courage*
    And went his way.
    To Sir Pilate, if he be wood,   *furious*
335   This dare I say.

   2 Sold.   Why, dar'st thou to Sir Pilate go
    With these tidings and say him so?
   1 Sold.   So rede I; if he us slo   *slay*
    We die but once.
340 *3 Sold.*   Now he that wrought us all this woe,
    Woe worth his bones!   *befall*

   4 Sold.   Go we then, sir knights hend,
    Since that we shall to Sir Pilate wend;   *must*
    I trow that we shall part no friend
345   Ere that we pass.
   1 Sold.   And I shall him say ilk word till end,
    Even as it was.

324 Yes, I strongly advise it, as I hope to prosper.
344–5 I don't think we shall part on friendly terms by the time we leave.
347 Exactly as it happened.

[SCENE III.   *The Judgment Hall*]

  1 Sold.   Sir Pilate, prince withouten peer,
      Sir Caiaphas and Annas in fere,
350   And all ye lordings that are here
      To neven by name,
      God save you all, on sides sere,   *everywhere*
      From sin and shame!

  Pil.   Ye are welcome, our knights keen.   *bold*
355   Of mickle mirth now may ye mean;   *speak*
      Therefore some tales tell us between,   *meanwhile*
      How ye have wrought.
  1 Sold.   Our waking, lord, withouten ween,   *vigil; doubt*
      Is worthed to nought.

360 *Cai.*   To nought?   Alas, cease of such saw!
  2 Sold.   The prophet Jesus, that ye well know,
      Is risen and gone, for all our awe,
      With main and might.
  Pil.   Therefore the devil himself thee draw,
365   False recrayed knight!   *recreant*

      Cumbered cowards I you call—   *beaten*
      Have ye let him go from you all?
  3 Sold.   Sir, there was none that did but small   *little*
      When that he yede.
370 *4 Sold.*   We were so feared, down gan we fall,   *frightened*
      And dared for dread.

  Ann.   Had ye no strength him to gainstand?   *oppose*
      Traitors! ye might have bound in band   *bonds*
      Both him and them that ye there found,

---

   351 To name, i.e. not forgetting.   (He is probably addressing these words to the audience.)
   359 Has come to nothing.
   362 For all his fear of us.
   364 *draw*, drag (with reference to the dragging of criminals to the place of execution).
   371 Cowered with fright.

375 And ceased them sone.
   1 Sold.   That deed all earthly men livand   *living*
   Might not have done.

   2 Sold.   We were so rad everilkone,   *frightened*
   When that he put beside the stone,   *aside*
380 We were so stonied we durst stir none,   *stupefied*
   And so abashed.   *confounded*
   Pil.   What! rose he by himself alone?
   1 Sold.   Yea, sir, that be ye trust.

   4 Sold.   We heard never since we were born,
385 Nor all our fathers us beforn,
   Such melody, midday ne morn,
   As was made there.
   Cai.   Alas, then are our laws lorn   *ruined*
   For evermore!

390 *2 Sold.*   What time he rose good tent I took,
   The earth that time trembled and quook;   *quaked*
   All kindly force then me forsook   *natural*
   Till he was gone.
   3 Sold.   I was afeard: I durst not look,
395 Ne might had none;

   I might not stand, so was I stark.   *stiff*
   Pil.   Sir Caiaphas, ye are a cunning clerk.   *learned*
   If we amiss have ta'en our mark,
   I trow sam fail;
400 Therefore what shall worth now of this work
   Say your counsel.

   Cai.   To say the best forsooth I shall,
   That shall be profit to us all:
   Yon knights behoves their words again-call   *revoke*

----

375 And stopped them at once.
383 You may be sure of that.
390 When he arose I noticed particularly.
395 Nor had I any strength.
398–401 If we have taken aim wrongly, I believe we shall both miss the mark; therefore say what you think will come of all this.

405   How he is missed;
       We nold, for thing **that might befall,**
       That no man wist.

    Ann.   Now, Sir Pilate, since that it is so
       That he is risen dead us fro,
410   Command your knights to say, where they go,   *wherever*
       That he was ta'en
       With twenty thousand men and mo,   *by*
       And them near slain.   *themselves*

       And thereto, of our treasury
415   Give to them a reward forthy.   *therefore*
    Pil.   Now of this purpose well pleased am I;   *plan*
       And further, thus:
       Sir knights, that are in deeds doughty,
       Take tent to us,   *pay heed*

420   And harken what that ye shall say
       To ilka man both night and day:
       That ten thousand men in good array
       Came you until,   *unto you*
       With force of arms bore him away
425   Against your will.

       Thus shall ye say in ilka land;
       And thereto, on that same covenant,
       A thousand pounds have in your hand
       To your reward;   *as*
430   And friendship, sirs, ye understand,
       Shall not be spared.

    Cai.   Ilkone, your state we shall amend;
       And look ye say as we you kenned.
    I Sold.   In what country so ye us send,   *whatever*

    406–7 On no account do we want anyone to know.
    409 That he has risen from the dead [and gone] from us.
    427 And also, under that same agreement.
    432–3 We shall improve the condition of each one of you; and see that
you say as we have instructed you.

435 By night or day,
Whereso we come, whereso we wend,
So shall we say.

Pil. Yea, and whereso ye tarry in ilk country,
Of our doing in no degree
440 Do that no man the wiser be,
Ne frain beforn;
Ne of the sight that ye gan see,   *did*
Neven it neither even ne morn.   *mention*

For we shall maintain you alway,
445 And to the people shall we say
It is greatly against our law
To trow such thing;
So shall they deem, both night and day,
All is leasing.   *a lie*

450 Thus shall the sooth be bought and sold,
And treason shall for truth be told;   *taken*
Therefore, ay in your hearts ye hold   *hold ye*
This counsel clean.   *wholly*
And fare now well, both young and old,
455 Wholly bedene.

439–41 See that no man is any the wiser about what we have done, or
questions you about it.
455 The whole lot of you.

THE JUDGMENT

The *Judgment*, as acted by the mercers of York and the weavers of Chester, is the concluding pageant of all the English cycles. Starting with the Creation and ending with the general Judgment, the medieval playwrights have dramatized the most significant scriptural events in which they believed God's purpose for mankind is revealed. Everything that has gone before has prepared us for the end, and so it is not surprising to find that the *Judgment* is full of echoes of earlier pageants. The Father of heaven has sent His Son to redeem Adam's race and to bridge the gulf between Himself and sinful mankind. On the day of doom those who have accepted Christ will be saved, and those who have rejected Him will be damned. This is the terrifyingly simple end of the long and troubled story of man's relations with God.

The simplicity and majesty of the Judgment are portrayed not only in the drama but in all the visual arts of the Middle Ages: sometimes magnificently, as in the great east window of York Minster, and sometimes crudely, as in the wall-paintings of many ancient parish churches.

The York *Judgment* is written in octaves, with alternate rhymes. Alliteration is used, but as occasional ornament and not to emphasize stressed syllables.

CHARACTERS

GOD

THREE ANGELS	JESUS
TWO GOOD SOULS	TWO APOSTLES
TWO BAD SOULS	THREE DEVILS

THE JUDGMENT

[Scene I. *Heaven*]

God. First when I this world had wrought—
Wood and wind and waters wan,   *dark*
And all kin thing that now is aught—
Full well, methought, that I did then;
5   When they were made, good me them thought.
Sithen to my likeness made I man,   *afterwards*
And man to grieve me gave he nought;
Therefore me rues that I the world began.

When I had made man at my will,
10 I gave him wits himself to wis;   *guide*
And Paradise I put him till,   *into*
And bade him hold it all as his.
But of the tree of good and ill
I said, 'What time thou eatest of this,
15 Man, thou speedest thyself to spill;
Thou art brought out of all thy bliss.'

Belive broke man my bidding.   *quickly*
He wend have been a god thereby;   *thought to*
He wend have witten of all kin thing,   *known*
20 In world to have been as wise as I.
He ate the apple I bade should hang;
Thus was he beguiled through gluttony.
Sithen both him and his offspring
To pine I put them all forthy.

25 Too long and late methought it good
To catch those caitiffs out of care;   *snatch; misery*

3 And every kind of thing that now exists at all.
5 I thought them good.
7–8 And man cared nothing about offending me; therefore I regret that
I created the world.
15 You will succeed in destroying yourself.
24–5 I put them all in torment therefore.   At long last I thought it good.

191

I sent my Son, with full blithe mood,
To earth to salve them of their sore.   *heal; pain*
For ruth of them he rest on rood,   *cross*
30   And bought them with his body bare;   *redeemed*
For them he shed his heart and blood.
What kindness might I do them more?

Sithen, afterward, he harrowed hell,
And took out those wretches that were therein;
35   There fought that free with fiends fele   *noble (one); many*
For them that were sunken for sin.
Sithen in earth then gan he dwell;   *did*
Ensample he gave them heaven to win,   *example*
In temple himself to teach and tell,
40   To buy them bliss that never may blin.   *obtain; cease*

Sithen have they found me full of mercy,
Full of grace and forgiveness;
And they as wretches, witterly,   *truly*
Have led their life in litherness.   *wickedness*
45   Oft have they grieved me grievously:
Thus have they quit me my kindness;   *repaid*
Therefore no longer, sikerly,   *certainly*
Thole will I their wickedness.   *suffer*

Men see the world is but vanity,
50   Yet will no man beware thereby;
Ilka day their mirror may they see,   *every*
Yet think they not that they shall die.
All that ever I said should be
Is now fulfilled through prophecy;
55   Therefore now is it time to me   *for*
To make ending of man's folly.

I have tholed mankind many a year   *allowed*
In lust and liking for to lend;
And uneaths find I far or near   *hardly*
60   A man that will his miss amend.   *wrongdoing*

36 For those who had sunk [down to hell] because of their sin.
39 Teaching and speaking in the temple.
50 Take warning by it.
58 To dwell in pleasure and delight.

On earth I see but sins sere;
Therefore my angels will I send
To blow their bemes, that all may hear   *trumpets*
The time is come I will make end.

65   Angels, blow your bemes belive,   *quickly*
Ilka creature for to call!
Lered and lewd, both man and wife,   *learned; unlearned*
Receive their doom this day they shall,   *judgment*
Ilka lede that ever had life;   *person*
70   Be none forgotten, great ne small.   *shall be*
There shall they see the wounds five
That my Son suffered for them all.

And sunder them before my sight!   *separate*
All sam in bliss shall they not be.   *together*
75   My blessed children, as I have hight,   *promised*
On my right hand I shall them see;
Sithen shall ilka waried wight   *accursed creature*
On my left side for fearedness flee.   *terror*
This day their dooms thus have I dight   *decreed*
80   To ilka man as he hath served me.

1 Angel. Lofed be thou, Lord, of mights most,
That angel made to messenger!   *as*
Thy will shall be fulfilled in haste,
That heaven and earth and hell shall hear.

[*He blows his horn.*

85   Good and ill, every ilka ghost,
Rise and fetch your flesh, that was your fere,   *companion*
For all this world is brought to waste.
Draw to your doom; it nighs near.

2 Ang. Ilka creature, both old and young,
90   Belive I bid you that ye rise;
Body and soul with you ye bring,
And come before the high justice.

61 Nothing but manifold sins.
81 Praised be thou, Lord, greatest in might.
85 Every single soul.

For I am sent from heaven king
To call you to this great assize;
95 Therefore rise up and give reckoning
How ye him served upon sere wise.

[*The dead rise up*]

1 Good Soul. Lofed be thou, Lord, that is so   *praised*
  sheen,   *radiant*
That on this manner made us to rise,
Body and soul together, clean,   *wholly*
100 To come before the high justice.
Of our ill deeds, Lord, thou not mean,
That we have wrought upon sere wise,
But grant us for thy grace bedene   *straightway*
That we may won in paradise.   *dwell*

105 *2 Good Soul.* Ah, lofed be thou, Lord of all,
That heaven and earth and all has wrought,
That with thy angels would us call
Out of our graves, hither to be brought.
Oft have we grieved thee, great and small;
110 Thereafter, Lord, thou deem us nought,
Ne suffer us never to fiends to be thrall,
That oft in earth with sin us sought.   *persecuted*

1 Bad Soul. Alas, alas, that we were born!—
So may we sinful caitiffs say.
115 I hear well by this hideous horn
It draws full near to doomsday.
Alas, we wretches that are forlorn,   *damned*
That never yet served God to pay,
But oft we have his flesh forsworn,   *abjured*
120 Alas, alas, and welaway!

96 In different ways.
101 Do not speak.
110 Do not judge us, Lord, accordingly.
118 Who have never yet served God so as to please Him.

What shall we wretches do for dread,
Or whither for fearedness may we flee,
When we may bring forth no good deed
Before him that our judge shall be?
125 To ask mercy us is no need,
For well I wot damned be we.
Alas, that we such life should lead
That dight us has this destiny.

Our wicked works they will us wry,   *accuse*
130 That we weened never should have been   *thought*
    witten;   *known*
That we did oft full privily,   *those that*
Apertly may we see them written.   *openly*
Alas, wretches, dear mun we buy!
Full smart with hell fire be we smitten;   *severely*
135 Now mun never soul ne body die,
But with wicked pains evermore be beaten.

Alas, for dread sore may we quake!   *sorely*
Our deeds be our damnation.
For our miss meaning mun we make;
140 Help may no excusation.   *excuse*
We mun be set for our sins' sake   *put*
Forever from our salvation,
In hell to dwell with fiends black,
Where never shall be redemption.

145 2 *Bad Soul.* As careful caitiffs may we rise;   *sorrowful*
Sore may we wring our hands and weep!
For cursedness and for covetise   *wickedness; covetousness*
Damned be we to hell full deep.
Recked we never of God's service,
150 His commandments would we not keep;
But oft then made we sacrifice
To Satanas when others sleep.

125 We need not ask for mercy.
127–8 Alas, that we led such a life that this fate was ordained for us.
133 We must pay dearly for them!
139 For our wrongdoing we must make lament.

Alas, now wakens all our were!   *fear*
Our wicked works may we not hide,
155   But on our backs us must them bear;   *we*
They will us wry on ilka side.
I see foul fiends that will us fear,   *frighten*
And all for pomp of wicked pride.
Weep we may with many a tear;
160   Alas, that we this day should bide!   *endure*

Before us plainly be forth brought   *shall be*
The deeds that us shall damn bedene.
That ears have heard or heart has thought,   *that which*
Since any time that we may mean;   *remember*
165   That foot has gone or hand has wrought;
That mouth has spoken or eye has seen—
This day full dear then be it bought.
Alas, unborn and we had been!

[*The Angel separates the Good Souls from the Bad*]

3 Ang.   Stand not together!   Part you in two!
170   All sam shall ye not be in bliss.   *together*
Our Father of heaven will it be so,   *wishes*
For many of you have wrought amiss.
The good, on his right hand ye go,
The way till heaven he will you wis;   *to; show*
175   Ye waried wights, ye flee him fro,
On his left hand, as none of his.

Jesus.   This woeful world is brought till end;
My Father of heaven he will it be.
Therefore till earth now will I wend,
180   Myself to sit in majesty.

167–8 This day it shall be paid for very dearly.   Alas, if only we had
never been born!
175 Ye accursed creatures, flee from Him.

To deem my dooms I will descend;
This body will I bear with me;
How it was dight, man's miss to mend,
All mankind there shall it see.

[*He descends to the earth.*

[SCENE II.   *The Judgment Seat of Christ*]

185 *Jesus.*   My apostles and my darlings dear,
The dreadful doom this day is dight.   *ordained*
Both heaven and earth and hell shall hear
How I shall hold that I have hight: *promised*
That ye shall sit on seats sere   *different*
190 Beside myself, to see that sight,
And for to deem folk far and near   *judge*
After their working wrong or right.   *according to; doing*

I said also, when I you sent
To suffer sorrow for my sake,
195 All tho that would them right repent
Should with you wend and winly wake;
And to your tales who took no tent   *words; heed*
Should fare to fire with fiends black.   *go*
Of mercy now may nought be meant,   *spoken*
200 But, after working, wealth or wrake.

My highting wholly shall I fulfil;   *promise*
Therefore come forth and sit me by
To hear the doom of good and ill.
I Apostle.   I lof thee, Lord God almighty!
205 Late and early, loud and still,
To do thy bidding bain am I.   *ready*
I oblige me to do thy will   *bind myself*
With all my might, as is worthy.

181 To pronounce my judgments.
183 How it was treated, in order to atone for man's wrongdoing.
195–6 All those who would duly repent should go with you and joyfully
awake [from the dead].
200 But, according to their deeds, [they shall have] happiness or
adversity.
205 i.e. at all times and in all circumstances.

   2 *Apost.* Ah, mightful God, here is it seen   *mighty*
210 Thou wilt fulfil thy forward right,   *promise*
   And all thy saws thou wilt maintain.   *sayings*
   I lof thee, Lord, with all my might,
   That for us that have earthly been
   Such dignities has dressed and dight.
215 *Jesus.* Come forth! I shall sit you between,
   And all fulfil that I have hight.

   *Here He goes to the Seat of Judgment, with the singing
    of angels.*

[SCENE III. *Hell*]

   1 Devil. Fellows, array us for to fight,   *prepare*
   And go we fast our fee to fang. *possessions; seize*
   The dreadful doom this day is dight;
220 I dread me that we dwell too long.
   2 Dev. We shall be seen ever in their sight,
   And warily wait, else work we wrong;
   For if the doomsman do us right,   *judge; justice*
   Full great party with us shall gang.   *go*

225 *3 Dev.* He shall do right to foe and friend,
   For now shall all the sooth be sought.   *truth*
   All waried wights with us shall wend;
   To pain endless they shall be brought.

[SCENE IV. *The Judgment Seat of Christ*]

   Jesus. Ilka creature, take intent   *heed*
230 What bodword I to you bring: *message*
   This woeful world away is went,   *passed*
   And I am come as crowned king.
   My Father of heaven he has me sent
   To deem your deeds and make ending.
235 Come is the day of judgment;
   Of sorrow may ilka sinful sing.   *Sinful (person)*

  214 Has prepared and made ready such dignities.
  221–2 We must always keep them in sight and watch warily, or else
we do wrong.
  234 End [all things].

The day is come of caitifness,   *misery*
All them to care that are unclean;   *bring care to*
The day of bale and bitterness,   *torment*
240   Full long abiden has it been;   *awaited*
The day of dread to more and less,
Of care, of trembling, and of teen,   *grief*
That ilka wight that waried is
May say, 'Alas, this day is seen!'

245   Here may ye see my wounds wide,
The which I tholed for your misdeed,   *suffered*
Through heart and head, foot, hand and hide,   *skin*
Not for my guilt but for your need.
Behold both body, back, and side,
250   How dear I bought your brotherhead!   *fellowship*
These bitter pains I would abide;   *endure*
To buy you bliss, thus would I bleed.

My body was scourged withouten skill;   *reason*
As thief full thraly was I threat;   *violently; threatened*
255   On cross they hanged me on a hill,
Bloody and blo, as I was beat,   *livid*
With crown of thorn thrusten full ill;   *pierced*
This spear unto my side was set;
My heart blood spared not they for to spill.
260   Man, for thy love would I not let.   *hinder (them)*

The Jews spit on me spitously;   *contemptuously*
They spared me no more than a thief.
When they me struck, I stood stilly;   *quietly*
Against them did I nothing grieve.
265   Behold, mankind, this ilk is I,   *same*
That for thee suffered such mischief;   *distress*
Thus was I dight for thy folly.   *treated*
Man, look, thy life was to me full lief.   *dear*

244 'Alas, that I have lived to see this day!'
264 I did not grow angry with them at all.

Thus was I dight thy sorrow to slake;   *assuage*
270   Man, thus behoved thee to borrowed be.
In all my woe took I no wrake;   *vengeance*
My will it was for the love of thee.
Man, sore ought thee to quake,
This dreadful day this sight to see.
275   All this I suffered for thy sake;
Say, man, what suffered thou for me?

                              [*To the Good Souls:*

My blessed children on my right hand,
Your doom this day ye thar not dread,   *need*
For all your comfort is comand;   *coming*
280   Your life in liking shall ye lead.
Come to the kingdom ay-lastand,   *everlasting*
That you is dight for your good deed.   *prepared*
Full blithe may ye be where ye stand,
For mickle in heaven shall be your meed.   *great; reward*

285   When I was hungry, ye me fed;
To slake my thirst your heart was free;   *generous*
When I was clotheless, ye me clad;
Ye would no sorrow upon me see;
In hard prison when I was stead,   *put*
290   Of my pains ye had pity;
Full sick when I was brought in bed,   *to*
Kindly ye came to comfort me.

When I was weak and weariest,
Ye harboured me full heartfully;   *sheltered; cordially*
295   Full glad then were ye of your guest,
And plained my poverty piteously;   *lamented*
Belive ye brought me of the best,   *quickly*
And made my bed full easily;   *comfortably*
Therefore in heaven shall be your rest,
300   In joy and bliss to be me by.

270 Thus it was necessary for your salvation.
273 You ought to tremble greatly.

1 Good Soul.   When had we, Lord that all has
  wrought,
  Meat and drink thee with to feed,   *food*
  Since we in earth had never nought
  But through the grace of thy Godhead?
305 *2 Good Soul.*   When was't that we thee clothes
  brought,
  Or visited thee in any need,
  Or in thy sickness we thee sought?
  Lord, when did we thee this deed?

 Jesus.   My blessed children, I shall you say
310 What time this deed was to me done:
  When any that need had, night or day,
  Asked you help and had it soon;
  Your free hearts said them never nay,
  Early ne late, midday ne noon,
315 But as oftsithes as they would pray, *often*
  Them thurt but bid, and have their boon.

       [To the Bad Souls:

 Ye cursed caitiffs of Cain's kin,
 That never me comfort in my care, *comforted*
 I and ye forever will twin,   *part*
320 In dole to dwell for evermore;   *grief*
 Your bitter bales shall never blin *cease*
 That ye shall have when ye come there;
 Thus have ye served for your sin, *deserved*
 For derf deeds ye have done ere. *wicked*

325 When I had mister of meat and drink, *need*
 Caitiffs, ye catched me from your gate; *chased*
 When ye were set as sirs on bink, *like; bench*
 I stood thereout weary and wet;
 Was none of you would on me think,
330 Pity to have of my poor state;
 Therefore till hell I shall you sink— *into*
 Well are ye worthy to go that gate. *way*

 316 They needed only to ask, and their request was granted.

	When I was sick and soriest,	*most sorrowful*
	Ye visited me not, for I was poor;	*because*
335	In prison fast when I was fest,	
	Was none of you looked how I foor;	*fared*
	When I wist never where for to rest,	*knew*
	With dints ye drove me from your door;	*blows*
	But ever to pride then were ye prest;	*inclined*
340	My flesh, my blood oft ye forswore.	

	Clotheless when I was oft, and cold,	
	At need of you, yede I full naked;	*in; went*
	House ne harbour, help ne hold	*shelter; support*
	Had I none of you, though I quaked;	
345	My mischief saw ye manifold;	
	Was none of you my sorrow slaked,	
	But ever forsook me, young and old;	
	Therefore shall ye now be forsaked.	

	1 Bad Soul. When had thou, Lord, that all thing has,	
350	Hunger or thirst, since thou God is?	*art*
	When was it thou in prison was,	
	When wast thou naked or harbourless?	
	2 Bad Soul. When was it we saw thee sick, alas?	
	When kid we thee this unkindness?	*showed*
355	Weary or wet to let thee pass,	
	When did we thee this wickedness?	

	Jesus. Caitiffs, as oft as it betid	*happened*
	That needful aught asked in my name,	*needy persons*
	Ye heard them not, your ears ye hid,	
360	Your help to them was not at home,	
	To me was that unkindness kid.	*shown*
	Therefore ye bear this bitter blame;	
	To least or most when ye it did,	
	To me ye did the self and the same.	

335 When I was bound fast in prison.
345 You saw my great distress.
355 To let thee go thy way weary or wet.

APPENDICES

I. The Cornish Trilogy

THE DEATH OF PILATE

The oldest example of the Cornish drama, preserved in a fifteenth-century manuscript, is a trilogy consisting of the *Origin of the World*, the *Passion of Our Lord*, and the *Resurrection*. These three plays, each of some three thousand lines, were intended to be acted on three consecutive days. The *Origin of the World* is the main source of the *Creation of the World with Noah's Flood*, which is in Cornish but with stage directions in English. The latter was copied by William Jordan in 1611 from a much older text, and is the only surviving play of a sequence resembling the extant Cornish trilogy. Cornish drama is also represented by a saint's play (*Life of Meriasek*), written in 1504.

The Cornish trilogy is particularly interesting because it dramatizes legends not found in the English cycles. The most remarkable of these is the legend of the Holy Rood and the Oil of Mercy, which is woven through the three plays of the trilogy. Another is the legend of the *Death of Pilate*, inserted between the *Pilgrims* and the *Ascension* in the last play of the trilogy.

The manuscripts of the trilogy and of *Meriasek* contain five circular diagrams illustrating the production of the plays; cf. the plan of the *Castle of Perseverance* (Introduction, p. xvi). These diagrams, together with the detailed stage directions, give a good idea of how the plays were presented in the circular playing-places or 'rounds,' two of which can still be seen at St Just and Perranzabuloe in Cornwall. Miracle plays were still being acted in Cornwall at the end of Elizabeth's reign, some years after the last performances of the English cycles.

The whole Cornish trilogy has been edited by Norris, and parts of it (the Rood legend, the *Three Marys*, and the *Death of Pilate*) have been done into English verse by Halliday, working from the unpublished translation of the Cornish plays by R. Morton Nance and R. S. D. Smith. The following literal rendering of the *Death of Pilate* into English is that of Norris (vol. ii, pp. 121–79), with some errors of translation corrected by J. Loth (*Revue Celtique*, xxvi. 261 ff.) and R. L. Thomson, and with extensive revisions made possible by the assistance of R. Morton Nance.

CHARACTERS

TIBERIUS CAESAR	FOUR EXECUTIONERS
COUNSELLOR	GAOLER
MESSENGER	SERVANT
PILATE	TRAVELLER
VERONICA	DEVILS

THE DEATH OF PILATE

The Death of Pilate begins, and Tiberius Caesar says:

TIBERIUS CAESAR

I am without equal above the people of the world,
But great is my sadness
That I am a leper.
What is best to be done?
If I cannot be cured,
I know not what I shall do.

COUNSELLOR

Lord, I seriously advise you
To send word to Pilate
By a messenger,
That he send you forthwith
Christ, King of the Jews,
On receiving word.

And He will cure you
Of every malady in this world,
As He is very God.
He is Lord of heaven and earth;
By Him thou shalt be healed,
Most truly indeed.

EMPEROR

My blessing on thee, counsellor!
Light-of-foot, my messenger,   [*To his Messenger.*
My good servant,
Thou must go an errand
For me immediately,
A little way from here.

MESSENGER

Lord Tiberius, by my hood,
Thou seest me, Light-of-foot,
Come to you.
What you want of me,
Tell me truly,
Immediately.

EMPEROR

Go to Pilate forthwith;
Christ, King of the Jews,
Who is God without equal,
Pray him that he send to me,
That he may have favour from me,
Tell him.

MESSENGER

O dear Lord, surely without delay
I will do thy errand.
I will not stay long with thee; farewell,
I say to thee.   [*He goes to Pilate.*

He says to Pilate:

Sir Pilate, joy to thee!
Through me thou art greeted
By Caesar the emperor.
To him take care that thou send
Christ, even to the door of his house,
As He is the flower of healers.

PILATE

Messenger, I pray thee go
Into the country and walk
A little while;
For if He is in the land
I will go and see,
Surely, myself.

And then the Messenger shall go and walk about in the
plain a little, and Veronica shall meet him.

VERONICA

Sweet young man who dost walk about,
I pray thee, whom thou seekest,
Tell me.

MESSENGER

What is that to thee?
Thou canst not help me,
Most truly, without doubt.

The emperor has sent me
To seek help in the country;
He suffers from leprosy,
He finds no doctor who can cure him.
Where Jesus is, I pray thee
To tell me;
He would cure him completely
Of every disease in this world.

VERONICA

Jesus, whom thou seekest, indeed
Is dead, gone to clay,
He who was our Lord;
And Pilate executed Him.
But that body, if it were living,
Would make the emperor
As well as ever he was,
However great his leprosy.

MESSENGER

Alas, that I ever came from home!
If that same body were living,
My lord would be cured.
Because my lord is so diseased,
O God, where shall I come, or where go?
I know not where I may set my foot.

VERONICA

I am one of his women,
And I will go to the emperor with thee;
And surely, in His name,
A remedy shall be made
That shall cure all his leprosy,
If he believes Him to be God of heaven.

MESSENGER

I shall rejoice at that!
So let us hasten to my lord.
If he can be healed,
Thou shalt have thy liberty,
And gold as thy guerdon:
Ever shall thy will be done.

[They go to the Emperor.

Sire, lord, be at ease!
That same prophet whom thou didst seek
Has been slain;
But a woman is with me
Who, through Him, will cure thee
Of thy affliction.

EMPEROR

Messenger, I will eat no food,
Because the prophet is dead
Who could surely have cured me.
O woman, what sayest thou?
Tell me if thou canst
In any point gladden me.

VERONICA

Believe in Christ, so I advise thee.
The print of His face I will show,
As He gave it me on a kerchief,
And as soon as thou seest Him,
He will heal thee, without other salve,
Of all thy leprosy.

EMPEROR

What is thy name, good woman?
Thou mayst find much favour,
If thy words be true;
And thou shalt be rewarded,
And be made a lady
Over much land, certainly.

VERONICA

My name is Veronica.
The face of Jesus is with me,
In a likeness made by His sweat;
And whoever sees it,
And believes in Him,
He must needs be healed.

In Christ thou must believe,
That He is Lord to us,
And salvation for the people of the world;
And healed thou shalt surely be
Of thy leprosy, if thou wilt
With full heart pray to Him.

EMPEROR

I will pray Him with full heart
To send health to me.
Even as thou art true God
And of great grace—
There is no Lord in the world
Save thee, truly I believe—
Help me in a short while
As thou art Saviour.

Show it to me, I pray thee;
That such a thing should be seen
Is a great wonder to me.
Come near to me, as thou lovest me,
For I would speak further indeed
With thee before parting.

VERONICA

Look at it, and in a short time
Thou shalt be cured of thy evil
Very quickly and easily.
Believe Him to be God of heaven,
And Saviour of all souls,
I tell thee.

> *Then she shall show him the kerchief, and he shall*
> *kneel, saying:*

EMPEROR

O Jesus, full of pity,
Thy dear face I will kiss;

> *He kisses the kerchief.*

I am sure that thou wilt cure me
Of all my leprosy;
O Lord Christ of heaven and earth,
Glory be to thee always!

> *He is healed of his leprosy.*

Now I am healed
Of all disease.

Lord, blessed be thou!
He who was our Lord,
Who is done to death,
There is no Lord above Him,
Either on earth or in heaven—
God without equal!

VERONICA

Now, since thou art healed,
Thou mayst know well
There is no God but He.
Pilate killed Him; without fail
Take vengeance on him,
For He was Christ, the King of heaven.

EMPEROR

Sweet Veronica, I will do it;
For through Him I am well,
Cured of all malady.
If he is in this world,
Most truly he shall go to death,
Both he and all who follow him.

Executioners, come to me,
Or surely retribution shall overtake you;
It shall be yours ere summer comes.
I have great distress
And sorrow in my heart;
I know not at all what I shall do.

[*Enter Executioners*]

FIRST EXECUTIONER

My lord, anon here we be.
To hear you was most horrible,
For you cried out so mightily;
And when you called us,
I thought I would die of fright—
I trembled!

EMPEROR

Go, seek Pilate for me.
Mind you are not wanting;
You are men of account.
Bring him to me, that I may see him;
He shall be put to death, if I find him,
Immediately.

SECOND EXECUTIONER

Let us go hence, and make haste
To seek that same fellow—
Detestable scum!

Bad man he ever was, surely;
To do evil he had no shame
In all his days.

THIRD EXECUTIONER

Dear lord, in a short time
To you he shall be brought,
Though he be so strong.
I will let nothing stop me:
Hither we will bring him;
He shall not withstand us.

[They go to Pilate.

FOURTH EXECUTIONER

Thou, Pilate, come to my lord!
Though thou refuse
Us now,
With us thou shalt certainly go,
Despite thy mother's son,
O false knave.

PILATE

I will not hesitate to go with you;
I will gladly go to my lord,
Tiberius Caesar.
Gentle he is to every one;
In my heart, indeed,
I love him greatly.

[They go to the Emperor.

FIRST EXECUTIONER

Lord, see the fellow here.
As you have heard, he tortured
And condemned the prophet Jesus
To be put upon the rood-tree,
And upon it He died;
On His body He suffered
Truly many pains,
To save the race of sons of men.

The Emperor comes down.

EMPEROR

O Pilate, thou art most welcome!
For I love thee, as God is my witness,
When I see thee.
As I say, at this time
I have no wish to harm thee;
Never shall I wish to do so.

PILATE

O lord, great thanks to you!
To you surely I have shown
How much I love.
On the earth thou hast no peer;
Gentle thou art of thy words,
Thou art a man without equal.

SECOND EXECUTIONER

Is it for this that we were
Bringing the fellow to you,
Indeed, so quickly—
For him to be put so much at ease?
Thou fellow, come out with us
Immediately.

They hold him.

THIRD EXECUTIONER

Out with us thou shalt go;
For a charm thou hast—
Tell us if thou art a sorcerer—
So that no man can do thee harm,
Either workday or Sunday.
Answer without more ado!

He shall let him go, and he retires to no great distance.

FOURTH EXECUTIONER

I think we might venture
At once, in my judgment, to kill him;
For, by my cloak,

I will tell you how it is:
The matchless body, by my father,
He has destroyed.

> *Here the Executioners absent themselves for a short time.*

EMPEROR

Out, out, out! harrow, harrow!
If Pilate be not slain,
I know not what I shall do.
He shall pay for it, the hateful fellow!
My heart for sorrow
Has indeed grown very sick.

When the foul fellow came forward,
He spoke cheerfully:
He made me give way.
In his answer I found
No fault at any time,
Or cause to kill him.

I believe the fellow is
A wizard and a great sorcerer:
There is not his like in the land,
Upon my soul!
Tell me, Veronica,
What is the best plan,
As thou lovest me, in this case,
At once without delay.

VERONICA

If he comes into your sight,
You can do him no harm,
I firmly believe;
As long as there is about him
The garment of Jesus, who hung on the rood-tree,
He will not be destroyed.

That is his undermost garment;
And yet bring him here
Again to you,

And strip it from him,
Or else you will do no harm to him
Ever.

EMPEROR

My blessing to thee, Veronica!
Since it is so,
I will get the garment.
Executioners, come to me forthwith,
That my heart may be lightened,
That we may not fail in what we do.

[*Enter Executioners*]

FIRST EXECUTIONER

Lord, behold us with you.
As we have often fared well
In your household,
Tell us your mind's desire,
And we will do it immediately,
Even as we should.

EMPEROR

Again bring Pilate to me;
As I was careless in dealing with him,
I was deceived.
For he is certainly an evil fellow;
By my faith, I hate him much,
The dirty stinkard!

SECOND EXECUTIONER

I will bring him to you without delay.
If we dare knock him
All to pieces,
We will no doubt do it to him;
But whoever sees him, loves him
In his heart.

THIRD EXECUTIONER

However much he may love him,
I don't mind killing him;
Never shall he sing in choir
With his mouth.
Behold him now taken!   [*He arrests Pilate.*
Come to my lord immediately,
And soon thou shalt be sentenced
To cruel punishment.

PILATE

I go to him joyfully,
As he is a powerful lord
And a noble man,
Very truly, and of great grace;
Emperor over many lands
He is, without doubt.

[*They go to the Emperor.*

FOURTH EXECUTIONER

Lord, look at the fellow.
I think, when you see him
Before you,
You will not be able to do him harm
While he is in your sight,
Most certainly.

EMPEROR

Executioners, all of you go to the city,
And see in every place
If anyone speaks against me.

[*Exeunt Executioners.*

Now, Pilate, I tell thee,
I'll take that robe without seam
Which is about thee, I will.

PILATE

You are a lord in rank;
The robe which I am wearing
Will certainly not do for you,

Nor is it for you to desire it:
It is not clean, but soiled;
I tell the truth.

It has not been washed a long time;
It would never do, by my faith,
For a lord like you.
I pray you,
Do not desire it
At this time from me.

EMPEROR

Pilate, I am not at all ashamed,
Certainly, of wearing the garment
Which was about Jesus.
Since I am anxious to have it,
I pray thee take it off quickly,
Without any more talk to me to-day.

PILATE

Lord, now if I take it off,
Before you naked I should be;
It would not be respectful to you,
Nor becoming
For a king or an emperor;
It would not be decent to see me.

VERONICA

Lord, command him
To take off the garment
Without another word;
For as long as you give way,
He will never take it off for you
At all.

EMPEROR

Take off the garment immediately,
For no longer shalt thou have respite
For any reason.

Seek not to parley with me any more;
I will have the robe,
Though thou grudge me it.

PILATE

Alas, since it must be taken off,
Henceforth there is no peace for me,
I know truly enough.   *[He takes the robe off.*
I do not see now that I can
Save my life, indeed,
Except by much gold.

EMPEROR

Out on thee, thou rascally fellow!
Thou hast killed Jesus,
My dear Lord.
Reach me my sword,
So that I may slay him,
As soon as the word.

VERONICA

Lord, that you shall not do!
Seek out the most cruel death
That he may have;
For the villain hath destroyed
That same Son who made us all,
Sea, earth, and heaven.

Thou shalt forthwith put him
Immediately in prison,
The hateful fellow,
Till he can be tried,
And be condemned by law
To death.

EMPEROR

Now into prison he shall go;
A cruel death like that
He shall have.
I will surely ordain for him
Hard punishment;
No man shall save him.

Ho, thou gaoler, come forth!
If thou come not, I will throttle thee,
And quickly!
Thou and thy boy, loiter not now;
My commands must be obeyed
Immediately.

[*Enter Gaoler and Servant*]

GAOLER

Lord, behold us ready.
What thou wishest to be done,
Tell me,
And we will straightway do it for thee,
At once without delay,
Whatever it be.

EMPEROR

Put this same fellow
Into a dungeon to rot,
That he may see no light at all;
He is a sorcerer.
The most cruel death there is
Will I ordain for him
That has slain Jesus, who was
To us a Saviour.

SERVANT

Lord, that will I do,
And put him in the lowest pit
Among vermin,
That he may suffer great torment.
A sprightly fellow is Whip-behind
At getting ideas!   [*He whips Pilate away.*

GAOLER

Take and cast him into prison!
Do not spare him, though he make an uproar;
He is a blockhead.

No idle threats, for he shall surely go;
He shall not escape, for all his cunning,
Without harm befalling him.

SERVANT

Now here thou shalt stay
Until all thy flesh rots.
When thou art sentenced,
Thou shalt have a hard death:
Well hast thou deserved it,
Thou art worse than a dog.

PILATE

Tell me, by your faith,
What death I shall have
That is decreed for me.
I well know I shall die:
Great is my anxiety,
Distressed am I!

GAOLER

The cruellest death there is,
By my faith, thou shalt have;
It is decreed for thee.
In this world trust no more;
Short are thy days,
Believe nothing else.

PILATE

From that will I yet preserve myself,
So that no man in the world may
Give me a cruel death;
For my own heart
With my knife I will pierce—
Oh! alas and welaway!   [*He stabs himself and dies.*

[*The Emperor's court*]

EMPEROR

Veronica, as thou lovest me,
I pray thee that thou say
What death would be best

To give the rascally fellow,
That he may suffer dreadful pain,
And die of injuries.

VERONICA

To make trial, my dear lord,
Ask the gaoler,
First of all, what plight he is in.
In truth, I believe,
Whatever pain is in the world
Would never be too much for him.

[Enter Gaoler and Servant]

EMPEROR

Gaoler, be thou right glad!
In what plight is Pilate
In the place where he is,
And what does he look like?
Tell me truly
How he is.

GAOLER

My lord, Pilate is dead:
Through pain and sorrow
He stabbed himself.
With his knife wondrous suddenly
He smote himself to the heart;
A cruel death he found.

EMPEROR

Jesus, blessed be thou,
That thou hast willed to give the villain
The cruellest death in the world;
For a more cruel death, indeed,
Than to kill himself,
No man may find, I think.

Thou gaoler, forthwith, thou and thy boy,
Take him by the two feet,
And put him deep in the ground;

For I right well believe
Many a man's son in this world
Of his body will have fear.

GAOLER

Whip-behind, take the head;
By the feet I will drag him backwards
Into the grave.

SERVANT

Master, I will, by my rear!
Vengeance take him, amen,
And a bad end.

And then he shall be thrown out of the earth.

O sweet master, by my soul,
On my faith this is a devil
Accursed!
Out of the earth he has jumped;
For very fear I have exploded,
I tell thee.

GAOLER

When he came and leapt from the grave,
I fled exploding;
I took fright,
As I say, rush-head,
For he surely could not move himself,
Shut in as he was.

SERVANT

Very boldly let us go at once to him,
Let us put him into the grave again.
Black is his hue!
I believe he will stay in it,
If he be on God of heaven's side,
Or else he is a devil.

GAOLER

And if he be not on God's side,
It would take all the parish
To guard him
And lay him in the grave.
Let us put him in the earth again
Straightway, without delay.

*And then they shall put him in the ground, and he shall
be thrown up again.*

SERVANT

By my faith, he is a strong devil!
He will not stay a moment under ground;
He is a wicked man.
Certainly God and the saints love him not;
Let us go and tell it to Caesar
At once, we two.

[*They go to Caesar.*

GAOLER

Sir Caesar, high lord,
The fellow will never stay
Under the ground.

EMPEROR

I knew it indeed!
He was a devil before he died,
Within the world.

SERVANT

When we put him in the grave,
Some bedevilment
Seized us,
And threw him up at once,
And the earth parted over him,
Dreadful to hear.

EMPEROR

Oh! out, out, out! what shall I do,
If against the devil I find
No shift in any way?
Unless Christ helps, indeed,
He will kill with stench
All my kingdom.

VERONICA

My lord, in a box of strong iron
In the river Tiber he shall stay
For his wickedness;
And from there certainly
He will nevermore come up
Until the day of doom.

EMPEROR

O Veronica, by my faith,
A counsel good and perfect
Thou hast given me.
Executioners, come hither quickly!
I almost get my death
Waiting for you.

[Enter Executioners]

FIRST EXECUTIONER

Lord, coming from Spain,
I was in the middle of Germany,
Eating a meal,
Most truly, when I was called.
Make known thy will, I pray thee,
Directly to us.

SECOND EXECUTIONER

Tell us the reason
Why you want us;
We are no loafers.
If there is sorrow in thy heart,
Thy will shall be done straightway
And speedily by us.

EMPEROR

Take the body of the wicked fellow,
Which is stinking with a tang
That is accursed.
Cast it, in a box of iron,
Into the river Tiber, in some creek
That it be sunk.

THIRD EXECUTIONER

At once the accursed fellow
In a trunk of iron shall be cast
Into Tiber, in very deep water;
Then there will be no need for us,
Or any man indeed,
Ever to fear again.

FOURTH EXECUTIONER

It is a most accursed body;
The water will not allow it
Within it, assuredly.
It is bedevilled;
May the fire of the great devil burn it,
That it come no more into the country.

FIRST EXECUTIONER

See, I have the iron box!
Put your two hands
On the coffin
With the accursed body in it;
To the water we must run with it
Like madmen.

SECOND EXECUTIONER

Behold the body laid in the box!
Carry it immediately
To a creek of the river.
Evil though his flesh was,
Never will I flinch from dragging it
Surely, for gold.

THIRD EXECUTIONER

The devil carry him to his place!
The body yet accursed
It is, most truly.
Let us go with him at great speed;
To put him into green water
Is my desire.

[*They bring Pilate's body to the Tiber.*

FOURTH EXECUTIONER

Go, thou cursed Pilate!
There in the water to the bottom
Surely thou shalt go,
And with thee the curses of all the parish
For falsely sentencing the Son of God,
The Son of Mary.

And then the body shall be thrown into the water.
[*Exeunt Executioners and enter a Traveller.*

TRAVELLER

So that I shall look my best,
Go and wash my hands
Straightway
Will I, here in the water,
That they may be white, and free
From dirt.

And he shall wash his hands, and shall die immediately.

Alas, that I was born!
Death surely is come
Suddenly to me.
I have no longer to live:
The water has done that for me,
Clearly enough.

A Messenger says to the Emperor:

MESSENGER

My lord, seek good advice:
No man goes over Tiber water,
Truly, without being killed.

It destroys many persons;
Put Pilate away from there,
For Jesus' sake, to another place.

EMPEROR

Out, out, out! what shall I do?
Except through thee, Veronica,
I shall have no help.
The body is accursed;
Give me counsel immediately,
That I may have peace.

VERONICA

As long as it is in the water,
No one goes over it without dying,
Man, woman, or beast:
It was an evil body in the world.
At once I advise thee,
Never be sad.

Whatever the cost in silver or gold,
Drag him out of the water,
Send him in a boat out to sea—
Buying it is no great matter;
The boat shall carry him to hell,
My lord, I warrant it.

EMPEROR

My blessing on thee, Veronica,
And the blessing of Mary's Son,
My dear Lord.
Executioners, come to me forthwith;
This way my heart may
Gladden me.

[Enter Executioners]

O arrant rogues, where were you?
It was terrifying, the noise
Of my shouting for you.
I know sorrow,
Gone now to my heart,
So God save me!

FIRST EXECUTIONER

I do not care to dally long,
Either workday or Sunday;
Hasten to say
What we must do.

EMPEROR

You must go without fail,
And drag Pilate up
Out of the water.
Send him in a boat out to sea,
And I will give you for that
Three millions in gold.

> [*The Executioners go again to the Tiber.*

SECOND EXECUTIONER

We'll drag him up immediately.
Great vengeance and a cruel fate
He asked for:
Jesus Christ, the King of heaven,
Him he judged, and falsely,
With very great injustice.

THIRD EXECUTIONER

Let us drag him from the water,
And earn our gold,
Comrades!
Let us cast a grappling-iron on him
Sharply, and lay hands on him,
That he may never escape.

FOURTH EXECUTIONER

I have cast two grappling-irons;
Out of the water the wicked
Body shall surely come,
Though it be heavy as stone.
Haul every man at once—
Have a care!

FIRST EXECUTIONER

May the devils fetch him!
See the hateful carcase
Coming up.
I tell you, forthwith
Let us drag him on to the grass,
The son of the evil one.

SECOND EXECUTIONER

Without further delay
We will put the body into a boat:
Straightway
Hustle it aboard,
With the curse of God and His angels,
And saints as well!

THIRD EXECUTIONER

See, it is afloat.
Go, hoist at once
Her sail,
That he may go with the wind,
And with him the curse of the saints,
And God above.

FOURTH EXECUTIONER

Now shove her off!
I hear a hideous noise
On a rock in the sea, and at his coming
The water is growing rough;
To my knowledge many devils
Are busy carrying him off.

FIRST EXECUTIONER

Let us hasten quickly to our country
From devils coming
For the spoil.
They are shouting gleefully:
Let us be off for fear of witchcraft,
At once, without delay.

[*Exeunt Executioners and enter Devils with Pilate's
    body.*

LUCIFER

My devils, come with me
All together, I pray you,
To fetch, with his soul,
The body of Pilate with great speed.
In roaring fire he shall remain,
And everlasting torment,
And his song shall be 'O woe is me,
That I was born into this world!'

BEELZEBUB

This body is accursed,
And so it falls to us;
It is not fit to be in earth,
Nor in water, nor in brine.

SATAN

In water of Tiber he was
Laid deep in a coffin of iron,
And a thousand lives he ended
In that water, for sorrow and fear.

BEELZEBUB

A ship never passed
This way, that was not drowned;
He deserved not bliss,
But to be overwhelmed with fire.

LUCIFER

From the water he was raised
And brought ashore again,
And put into a great ship,
To go down with us to the abyss.

SATAN

Sail and mast were made ready for him,
That he might go away from the land;
Upon a rock he was cast,
So that he fell into my toils.

BEELZEBUB

That rock opened,
As was fated for him,
For in truth he renounced
By his deeds the kingdom of heaven.
There we received him:
His voice is horrible to hear;
Fire and smoke and great heat
In that rock shall ever remain.

LUCIFER

Scorching heat and piercing cold,
Monstrous grimacing of devils
Shall he find with us,
And all evil kinds of torment.

SATAN

And thou, great cursed body,
To hell, with thy soul,
Shalt thou be dragged by us;
Thy song shall be 'Woe is me!'

BEELZEBUB

Now every one lend a hand
To drag him in this same boat.
And thou, Tulfric, a plain-chant
Begin to sing to us.

TULFRIC

Yah, kiss my rear!
For its end is out
Very long behind me.
Beelzebub and Satan,
You sing a great drone bass,
And I will sing a fine treble.

And so ends The Death of Pilate.

II. CONTENTS OF THE CYCLES

The following names of pageants comprising the Chester, York, and Towneley cycles are listed below for the purpose of showing the full range and content of the three cycles from which most of the pageants in this volume have been taken. The pageants included in this volume are marked with an asterisk.

CHESTER

Banns.
1. Fall of Lucifer (Tanners).
2. Creation and Fall; Death of Abel (Drapers).
3. *Noah's Flood (Water-leaders and Drawers in Dee).
4. Lot; Abraham and Isaac (Barbers and Wax-chandlers).
5. Balaam and his Ass (Cappers and Linen-drapers).
6. Salutation and Nativity (Wrights and Slaters).
7. Shepherds (Painters and Glaziers).
8. Coming of the Three Kings (Vintners).
9. Offering; Return of the Kings (Mercers).
10. Slaughter of the Innocents (Goldsmiths).
11. Purification (Blacksmiths).
12. Temptation; Woman Taken in Adultery (Butchers).
13. Lazarus (Glovers).
14. Christ's Entry into Jerusalem (Corvisors).
15. Betrayal of Christ (Bakers).
16. Passion (Fletchers, Bowyers, Coopers, Stringers).
17. Crucifixion (Ironmongers).
18. *Harrowing of Hell (Cooks and Innkeepers).
19. Resurrection (Skinners).
20. Pilgrims to Emmaus (Saddlers).
21. Ascension (Tailors).
22. Descent of the Holy Spirit (Fishmongers).
23. Ezechiel (Cloth-workers).
24. Antichrist (Dyers).
25. Judgment (Websters).

YORK

1. *Creation; Fall of Lucifer (Barkers).
2. Creation, to the Fifth Day (Plasterers).

3. *Creation of Adam and Eve (Cardmakers).
4. Adam and Eve in Eden (Fullers).
5. *Fall of Man (Coopers).
6. Expulsion from Eden (Armourers).
7. Sacrifice of Cain and Abel (Glovers).
8. Building of the Ark (Shipwrights).
9. Noah and his Wife; Flood (Fishers and Mariners).
10. Abraham and Isaac (Parchmenters and Bookbinders).
11. Departure of the Israelites from Egypt; Ten Plagues; Crossing of the Red Sea (Hosiers).
12. Annunciation and Visitation (Spicers).
13. Joseph's Trouble about Mary (Pewterers and Founders).
14. Journey to Bethlehem; Birth of Jesus (Tile-thatchers).
15. Shepherds (Chandlers).
16. Coming of the Three Kings to Herod (Masons).
17. Coming of the Kings; Adoration (Goldsmiths).
18. Flight into Egypt (Marshals).
19. Slaughter of the Innocents (Girdlers and Nailers).
20. Christ with the Doctors (Spurriers and Lorimers).
21. Baptism of Jesus (Barbers).
22. Temptation (Smiths).
23. Transfiguration (Curriers).
24. Woman Taken in Adultery; Lazarus (Capmakers).
25. Christ's Entry into Jerusalem (Skinners).
26. Conspiracy (Cutlers).
27. Last Supper (Bakers).
28. Agony and Betrayal (Cordwainers).
29. Peter's Denial; Jesus before Caiaphas (Bowyers and Fletchers).
30. Dream of Pilate's Wife; Jesus before Pilate (Tapiters and Couchers).
31. Trial before Herod (Litsters).
32. Second Accusation before Pilate; Remorse of Judas; Purchase of the Field of Blood (Cooks and Water-leaders).
33. Second Trial before Pilate (Tilemakers).
34. Christ Led to Calvary (Shearmen).
35. *Crucifixion (Pinners and Painters).
36. Mortification of Christ; Burial (Butchers).
37. Harrowing of Hell (Saddlers).
38. *Resurrection (Carpenters).
39. Christ's Appearance to Mary Magdalene (Winedrawers).
40. Travellers to Emmaus (Sledmen).
41. Purification of Mary; Simeon and Anna (Hatmakers, Masons, Labourers).
42. Incredulity of Thomas (Scriveners).

43. Ascension (Tailors).
44. Descent of the Holy Spirit (Potters).
45. Death of Mary (Drapers).
46. Appearance of Mary to Thomas (Weavers).
47. Assumption and Coronation of the Virgin (Hostlers).
48. *Judgment (Mercers).

TOWNELEY

1. Creation (Barkers of Wakefield).
2. Murder of Abel (Glovers).
3. Noah and his Sons (Wakefield).
4. Abraham and Isaac.
5. Isaac.
6. Jacob.
7. Prophets.
8. Pharaoh (Litsters).
9. Caesar Augustus.
10. Annunciation.
11. Salutation of Elizabeth.
12. First Shepherds' Pageant.
13. *Second Shepherds' Pageant.
14. Offering of the Magi.
15. Flight of Joseph and Mary into Egypt.
16. *Herod the Great.
17. Purification of Mary.
18. Pageant of the Doctors.
19. John the Baptist.
20. Conspiracy.
21. Buffeting.
22. Scourging.
23. Crucifixion.
24. Talents.
25. Harrowing of Hell.
26. Resurrection.
27. Pilgrims to Emmaus (Fishers).
28. Thomas of India.
29. Ascension.
30. Judgment.
31. Lazarus.
32. Hanging of Judas.